THE POLISH CANADIANS

© 1981, The Estate of the late William Kurelek

William Kurelek completed the 26 paintings for *The Polish Canadians* shortly before his death in 1977. The series was purchased by the Polish Alliance of Canada and presented as a gift to the Art Gallery of Hamilton, Ontario. Assisting with donations were Dofasco, The Great-West Life Assurance Company, John Kotowski, The Oblate Fathers of Assumption Province, the Marie Curie-Sklodowska Women's Club of Toronto; these contributions were matched by a grant from Wintario. The late Ted Glista was chairman of the project and arranged for the series to travel to Poland where it was exhibited at the Ethnographical Museum in Warsaw in June 1978 under the sponsorship of the Ministry of Culture of Poland and Polognia.

All rights reserved. No part of this work may be reproduced or transmitted in any form or by any means, electronic or mechanical, including photocopying and recording, or by any information storage or retrieval system, without permission in writing from the publisher.

Published in Canada by
Tundra Books of Montreal
Montreal, Quebec   H3G 1R4

Published in the United States by
Tundra Books of Northern New York
Plattsburgh, N.Y. 12901

Tundra Books Inc. has applied funds from its Canada Council block grant for 1981 toward the editing and production of this book. Assistance was also given toward the cost of making the color transparencies and separations by the Multiculturalism Program of the Government of Canada.

Design: Michael M. Cutler

Transparencies by T.E. Moore, Toronto. Color separations and printing Herzig Somerville, Toronto. William Kurelek is represented by the Isaacs Gallery, Toronto

Printed in Canada

ISBN 88776-131-3

Books by William Kurelek

A Prairie Boy's Winter
A Prairie Boy's Summer
Lumberjack
A Northern Nativity
Fields
Fox Mykyta
The Passion of Christ
Ukrainian Pioneers
Kurelek's Canada
The Last of the Arctic
Jewish Life in Canada
Who Has Seen the Wind
O Toronto
Someone With Me

Credits

In crediting help given toward the publication of this book, particular mention must be made of historian William Boleslaus Makowski of St. Catharines, Ontario. William Kurelek used material from his book *History and Integration of Poles in Canada*, 1967, The Canadian Polish Congress, as the basis for several paintings and texts, particularly where 19th and early 20th century activities were concerned. Mr. Makowski also assisted the present publisher in checking details.

Roman Malanczak of Toronto and Combermere, Ontario, who guided Kurelek through the Polish districts in the Barry's Bay area, also helped the publisher with additional information and suggestions.

All persons mentioned by name in the text who are now living were asked to check details relating to them or their family. The publisher is grateful for their immediate and friendly help. Others who assisted include Jean Kurelek and Marina Glista, both of Toronto, who sent information relating to their late husbands; Henry Lopinski, president of the Polish Alliance of Canada; Father J.A. Maclean of Sydney, N.S.; Dr. A.H. Chapeskie of Barry's Bay, Ontario; Peter Hamula of Edmonton; Pierre Berton; the Polish Institute Library and McGill University Library in Montreal; the Oblates de Marie-Immaculée in Montreal; the National Personnel Records Centre of the Public Archives in Ottawa; Father Ignatius Rafal Jan Grzondziel; Ambrose Lehovitch of Barry's Bay; Michael Pearson of the history department of the Metropolitan Toronto Library; Wycliffe College; Glen Cumming and the Art Gallery of Hamilton, Ontario.

THE POLISH CANADIANS
WILLIAM KURELEK

TUNDRA BOOKS

Introduction

It took some weighing of sensibilities against facts before I could arrive at this particular title for a pictorial history of Polish settlement in Canada. Poles always tended to be intensely patriotic. Like the Irish they left their homeland often against their will and so, whether they settled in Canada or the States, they usually thought of themselves first of all as Poles.

They are the fifth major pioneer group of Canada which I've chosen to illustrate. This series originated largely from my friendship with Roman Malanczak, a retired Toronto engineering draftsman. He helped in three main ways. First, he introduced me to Polish culture and traditions. Second, he took me on several tours of Kaszuby, the original large settlement of Poles in northern Ontario dating from 1864. And finally, once I'd selected the subjects for these paintings, he gathered reference materials for me to work from in the actual execution of them. Roman has his cottage in the Kaszuby district, and I my farm studio nearby, which contributed toward the authenticity of the series.

Our relationship has been a warm one because of Roman's artistic and philosophic sensitivity and because we share a common religious faith. However, being of Ukrainian origin, I found I could not share with him a common view of Polish-Ukrainian history. The two countries border on each other. So by mutual unspoken consent we've avoided the subject. In the Irish series I was able to include one painting on conditions in their homeland brought about, in large part, by English occupation which forced millions of Irish to emigrate. In this series, apart from mentioning in the notes that the Kaszuby settlement was motivated by oppressive Prussian land laws and that Sir Casimir Gzowski was a refugee from Russian suppression of the Polish revolt of 1831, I've avoided the Old Country. Since it's impossible to find a middle ground acceptable to both my Polish and Ukrainian friends it seems to me the best solution is to put that troubled past aside altogether here in Canada. We can share whatever of the Old Country cultural traditions we've managed to preserve here and the histories of our struggles to make good in this new land — in a word, to build a specifically Canadian relationship of mutual respect.

Besides Roman there are several other people who contributed to the making of this series and its exhibition: Michael Pearson, a Toronto central librarian, Adolf Piechowski, former township clerk in the Kaszuby district. Ted Glista, Frank Ritza, Doctor Elias Wachna and Henry Chapeskie, each contributed one story to illustrate. Geza and Sandy Takacs, my brother-in-law and sister, put the frames together. The Polish motif panels in them were done by John Pinto, my Indian friend, and Agnes McLaren. Ted Glista deserves special recognition. It was he who recognized the worth of the series as historical record and worked at preserving it intact by having the Polish Alliance of Canada buy the whole series. It was he also who arranged for the exhibit to travel to Poland. His interest and effort were a big incentive for me to go ahead with the series.

Last but not least I have to tell of the important contribution of actual painting made to this series by Nick Bidniak and Sylvia Chan. Nick, a Ukrainian painter, did most of Our Lady of Czestochowa in the outdoor chapel scene. Sylvia, my apprentice from China, worked on all the grass and leaves, shingles, wallpaper, etc., with me. I hope, therefore, it's obvious to all visitors to this exhibition how the different nationalities that make up this country can pitch in toward honoring one of their number.

William Kurelek, 1977

The dream they followed

The refugee as aristocrat

This painting gave me by far the most trouble in this series; partly because of all the work I foresaw in my original composition and partly because I felt out of class with this aristocratic man. Sir Casimir Stanislaus Gzowski came from the officer class of Poland and Russia and despite a period of hardship as a refugee he ended up in a class with royalty. Yet there was no way I could give up on the subject. I needed at least one painting to represent the individual Polish emigrant and refugee who came to Canada on his own during the 19th century before the group settlement of Poles in Canada began. The mark of such men on Canada was considerable, especially in Gzowski's case. Fortunately I hit on a surrealistic and symbolic approach and solved the painting problems that way.

The stance I've given him is that of one who has passed over the waters in the foreground and established himself successfully in the New World. Thus his new life is represented by the tree with ripe fruit and leafy branches. His old life in Poland lost because of his participation in the abortive Polish rebellion against Russian occupation in 1831 is represented by the broken, withered tree. In the far background I've indicated symbolically the many achievements of this competent, practical, yet cultured man. He seemed to have a compulsion to get involved in every social activity over and above his profession of engineering. On the horizon we see his major construction projects connected with the initial industrialization of Ontario: hydro power stations; waterfronts; railways; canals; bridges; mining; and the beautification of the province with parks.

Symbolically in fact, I've represented his great loyalty to the British crown by laying down the park in the middle ground in the form of a Union Jack. Queen Victoria took this loyalty into account when she appointed him Commander of the Order of St. Michael and St. George; he was thenceforth known as "Sir Casimir." He readily accepted the many honors bestowed on him and there are many portraits of him in ceremonial dress. One of these is of him as Colonel of the Reserves for he both commanded Canada's defence forces and built fortifications for them at the time of the Sinn Fein raids. He was a patron of music in the city of Toronto, where he lived and died. He was a founder of Wycliffe College and promoted sports there. All of these I've represented symbolically in the middle ground. W.K.

Sir Casimir Gzowski

William Kurelek

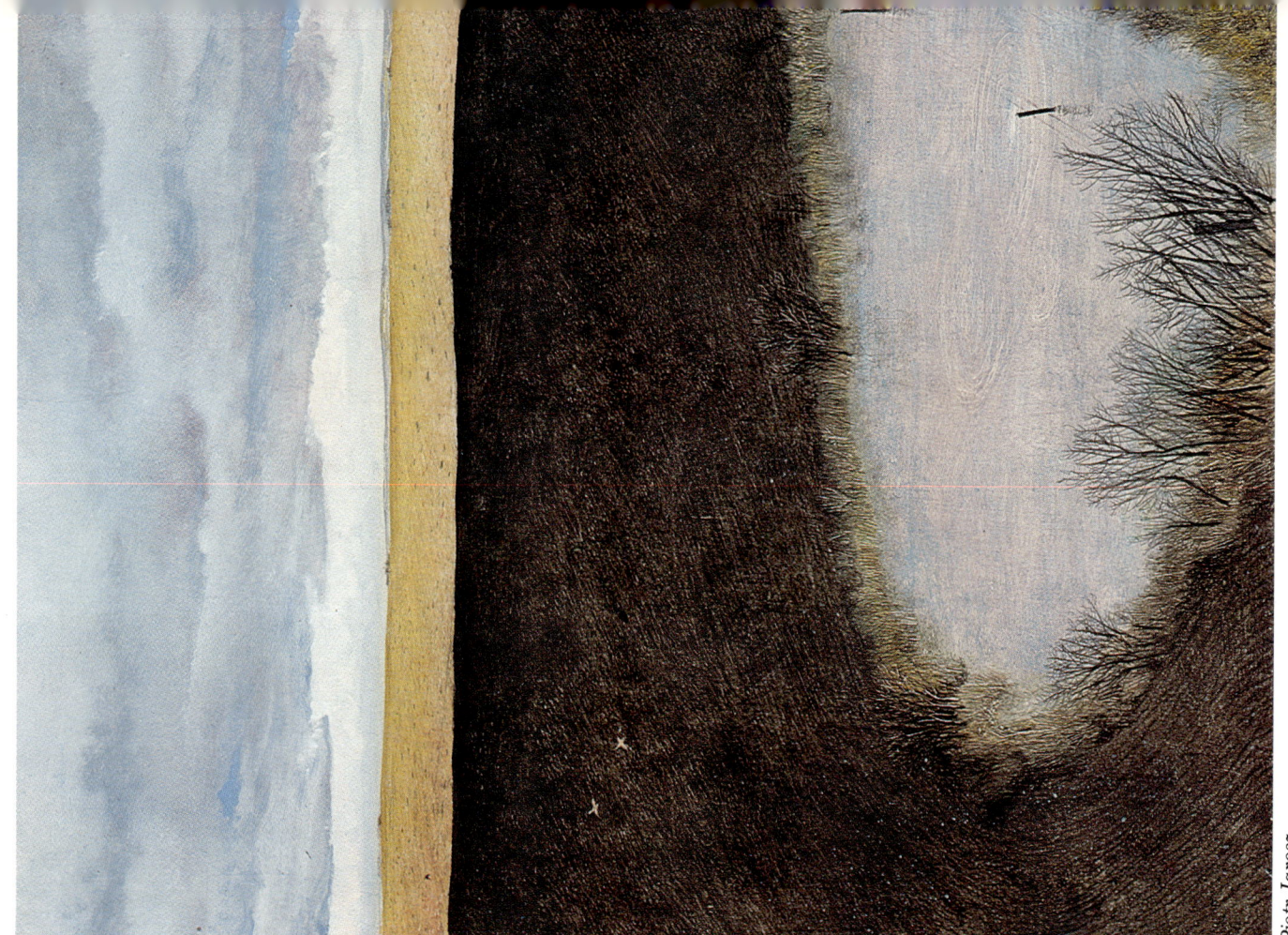

Piotr Jarosz

The long walk to Edmonton

This painting is deliberately the largest in the series as I've tried to convey some of the loneliness and harshness of homesteading in western Canada. We see Piotr Jarosz, an early homesteader, walking into Edmonton just barely visible on the horizon. I will paraphrase his memoirs as recorded by historian Makowski:

"... I arrived in Edmonton in 1911 and found work in the city sewer system digging ditches. I was paid 10¢ an hour and worked there for two years. After I'd saved $60 I bought myself a homestead near Rochester, 85 miles north of Edmonton. At the end of each month I walked there and back. My first house was a shack made of tree branches. The second house was still only one room but had a large fireplace in the middle of it.

"I still had to work outside to buy necessary tools and utensils for the farm and house. Putting in 10

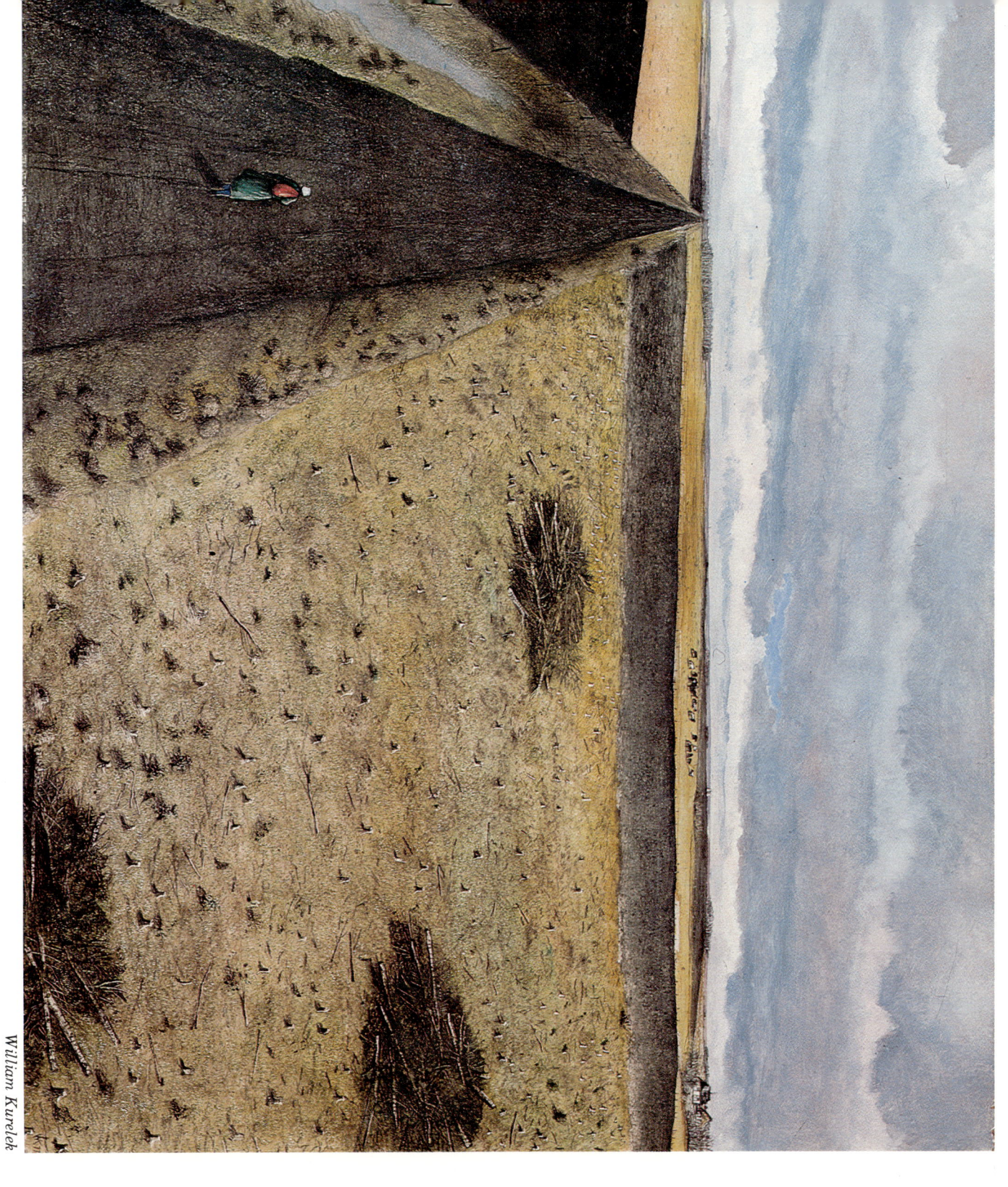

William Kurelek

hours a day, 25¢ per hour, I was able to save up enough at last to bring over from Poland in 1914 my wife, daughter and two small sons. We all lived in that one room while I continued to walk 85 miles into the city simply because there was no transportation.

"There were no schools either and the children learned only what their mother could teach them. All farm work was done by hand until 1917 when I saved enough to buy our first horse and a year later a second one. That same year we got our first cow too and when the railway came to Rochester we carried our farm produce there on our backs some eight miles distant. My daughter found employment as a domestic for six dollars a week and we saved four of these six dollars each week so I could repay the government the 60 dollars I'd borrowed from them..." W.K.

In stony, swampy forests

Oppressive Prussian land laws in the Polish province of Pomerania brought the local inhabitants, the Kaszubs, down to such a level of poverty and cultural rootlessness that they were prepared to emigrate anywhere for relief. The British Canadian government at that same time needed just such a people to populate the upper Ottawa Valley. The land was stony, swampy and heavily forested. But a populated corridor to western Canada was considered a must by British military strategists in case the more vulnerable population centers of the St. Lawrence and Niagara Peninsula should fall to the Americans. The Irish and Poles filled the role.

At first this painting may strike one as a romantic scene. But the mist rising off the lake waters, as it does to this day in the Renfrew area, and the moonlit sky belie the hardship and privation of pioneer life. I quote from the Bishop of Pembroke's diocesan handbook about those first weeks and months in the new land:

"... Now to find some kind of shelter and protection, for the family in this land of towering trees and prowling animals; The father found it not far from the trail ... a huge tree, that had been turned up at the roots by the wind. With the help of an axe he had purchased at Brudenell on his way in, a crude dwelling was soon in readiness. This would have to serve the purpose until, with the help of other settlers, a log shanty could be constructed.

"One can well imagine the inconveniences of living under such circumstances, even in the summer time. Swarms of mosquitoes filtered in through the bows and branches interlaced for walls. The pests were smoked out temporarily by a smudge and decoyed by a fire kept burning throughout the night some distance from the camp. Sometimes, too, it became a problem whether to brave the attacks of the flies, or have their eyes and throats scorched by the acid smoke blowing over them as they rested. Once, in a sudden windstorm, the brush and bark roof of their dwelling was lifted bodily and rolled away a hundred yards. The roof was not much use anyway, for the poor people were often drenched with passing rain showers.

"There were no tools to work with, only an axe and a hoe. Shovels were hewed out of maple, as were some of the platters to hold food. The first iron pot the father was able to obtain in Brudenell, occasioned great rejoicing in the family circle. They celebrated by making a porridge of pounded oats. After some weeks each had a plate of his own and graded according to the age of the owner. Mud turtle shells, after the meat was boiled out of them, made excellent plates and bowls ... " W.K.

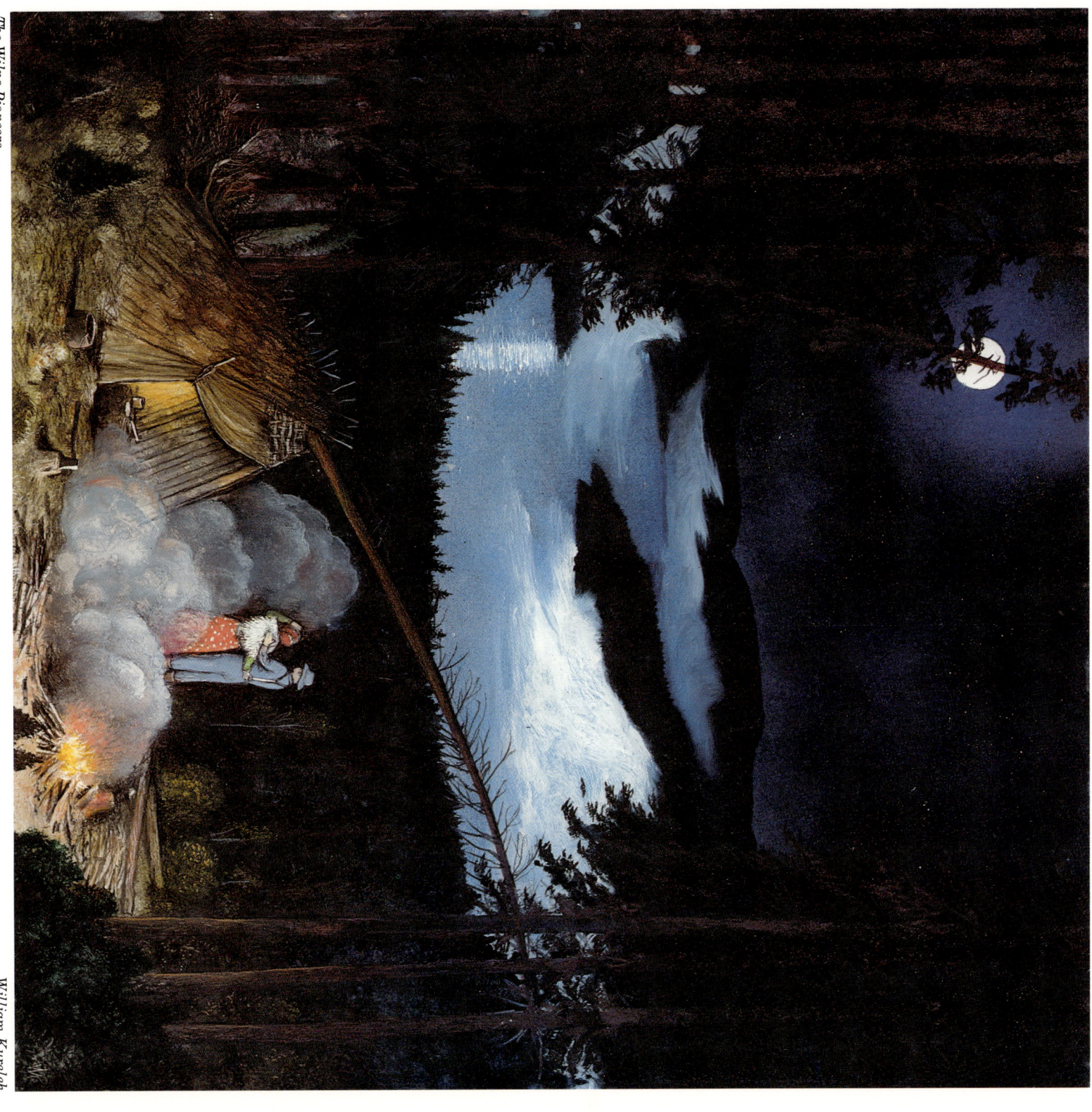

The Wilno Pioneers — William Kurelek

Part two

In the dark of grain elevators

Like the Ukrainian who immigrated to Canada in between the wars for economic reasons, many Poles also settled in Fort William and Port Arthur (now Thunder Bay) to work in the grain elevators, shipyards and railways. I once worked in those giant elevators myself, as a construction worker, rather than a handler of grain although I'd shoveled plenty of it on my father's farm. Our construction gang shared the union lunchrooms with the elevator workers and I gathered in conversations with the Poles that there was a considerable communist movement among them.

First of all the Poles, like other Slavic immigrants, experienced some discrimination at the time. This tended to turn them in on themselves and look to breaking out of their humiliation through radical liberation movements. It was also the time of the Great Depression. Management had the whip-end then, so to speak. Those who did have employment and families to support were always fearful of losing their jobs. In some cases, they submitted to bad working conditions from which they might have rebelled otherwise. I've used my own experience of grinding labor to depict these men topping off a grain bin under the watchful eye of a superintendent. Those are his feet in the clean air above. When these Poles got home after work and turned to their various fraternal organizations for social life, they found the struggle between left and right wing factions obvious there too. W.K.

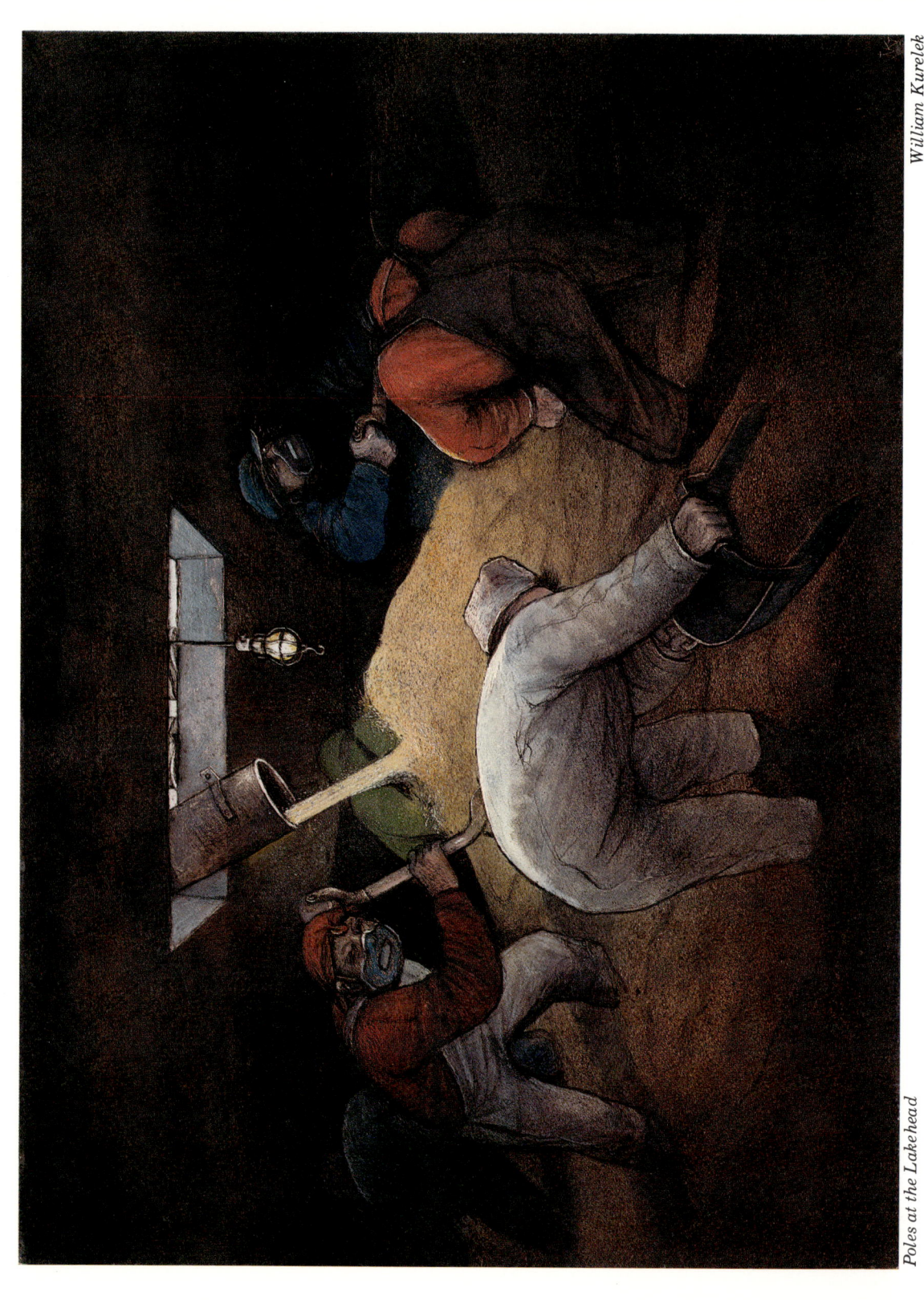

Poles at the Lakehead — *William Kurelek*

The work they did

With the help of a wife

Dr. Elias Wachna, a Toronto dentist, gave me this story.

The southeastern Manitoba border villages of Tolstoi, Gardenton and Sundown had some 6,000 Ukrainian settlers. Curiously, in each of those villages the blacksmith was Polish. In Wachna's hometown, Stuartburn, it was Frank Pawlowski.

These Poles got along well with their Ukrainian customers with whom they were able to speak their own language. They attended their own Roman Catholic church and even put up private roadside shrines. Socially they joined Ukrainians in festivities and were in demand as musicians.

The land in that area was often poor and stony and a blacksmith provided a valuable service repairing broken wheels, blades, disks, plows, as well as shoeing horses. This blacksmith shop had four main sections. Inside on the left were three horse stalls for shoeing. On the right, also in the front, was the main work area with a coal-fired hearth with air pumped by a crank and foot bellows. There traditionally stood the large black anvil, an assortment of sledgehammers of various sizes and half a barrel of water for tempering the hot iron. At the center of the shop was an eight-pulley gas-driven motor with belts leading to various machines, each for a different purpose such as drilling holes, polishing, sanding and spraying. The last area was for storage of bolts, nuts, steel rods, plates and spare parts.

Income was small from this service, so each blacksmith had to supplement his income from land where he raised horses, milk cows, chickens and tended a garden. Pawlowski's place was about 10 acres and was well planned with a two-story frame house, a new barn, fences and in front by the main road was the smith shop. The farm was near a valley blending to the beautiful fresh water of the Roseau River which the town enjoyed for swimming in the summer and skating in the winter. Pawlowski's wife and children usually looked after the farm and occasionally Frank's wife Klementina had to help in the shop, too. Their family had five daughters and one son. However, during a scarlet fever epidemic their young only son and a daughter died. The other girls grew up and went on to work as maids in Winnipeg and married happily.

Stuartburn in the years 1900 to 1925 was in the pre-car era and served as a central village. Besides the smith shop there was a sawmill, a flour mill which was three stories high, a post office, a church, a two-room school, a community hall and two stores were run by Mr. Rosenstock and Mr. Wachna. The police officer was a man named Frank Millar who learned to speak both Polish and Ukrainian. A western group of touring musicians provided entertainment. The town even had its own threshing machine which provided jobs at harvest for over 25 men.

I had no photos of that shop so I made this picture up using an Austrian one in Saskatchewan and a Polish shop in Barry's Bay for reference. W.K.

Frank and Klementina Pawlowski

William Kurelek

Cutting logs from giant trees

I interviewed Frank Ritza for this one. He is a retired sign painter and jack-of-all-trades in Barry's Bay. The NFB film "Kaszuby" opens with him talking about the village. Actually it was his father who was the lumberjack. His father never went to school — there were none then — and typical of those hard times, he went to work at the early age of 15 for the famous timber baron of the Ottawa Valley. In a short while he rose to be foreman of a camp of 110 men and he had a rough-tough reputation as a drinker and a fighter.

This picture is derived from a photo of Ottawa Valley lumbering. The pulp and paper industry was only in its infancy at the end of the last century. The virgin forest of the area, hundreds of years old, produced the size of logs seen in this painting. Today one sees plenty of timber trucks in the Barry's Bay area hauling logs to the many sawmills around. But these logs are puny in size compared to the size of their parent trees. The men in the photo could just as well have been Irish or French Canadian, the other two main nationalities of the Ottawa Valley. I myself never saw the cant hook in the picture when I was a lumberjack. But my "old timer" neighbors at Combermere, Frank Pastway, Adolf Piechowski's father and Frank Ritza all remember using them. W.K.

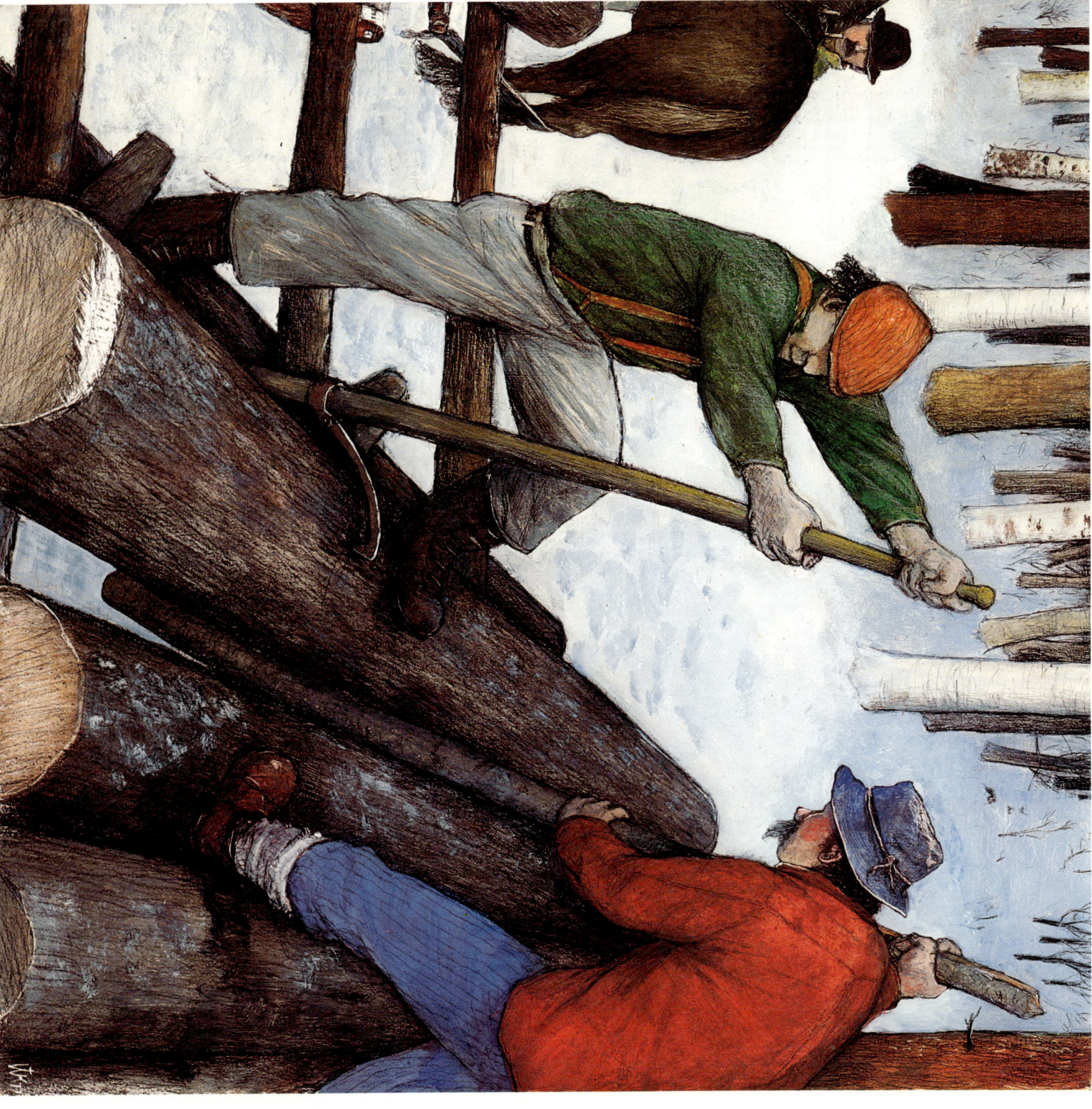

Polish lumberjacks in the Ottawa Valley — William Kurelek

Keeping the railway line open

The first transcontinental line was pushed through with labor other than Polish such as the Irish or Chinese because East European settlement in western Canada had not yet begun. But the C.P.R.'s branch lines and the next big transcontinental railway, the C.N.R., had many Poles laboring on them. Some were seasonal laborers, such as farmers making extra cash to buy livestock and implements for their homesteads. Others were permanent employees who could be found wherever hard work was appreciated such as the railway yards of the main railway centers across the country, or on section gangs, sometimes way out in the back country as depicted in this picture. W.K.

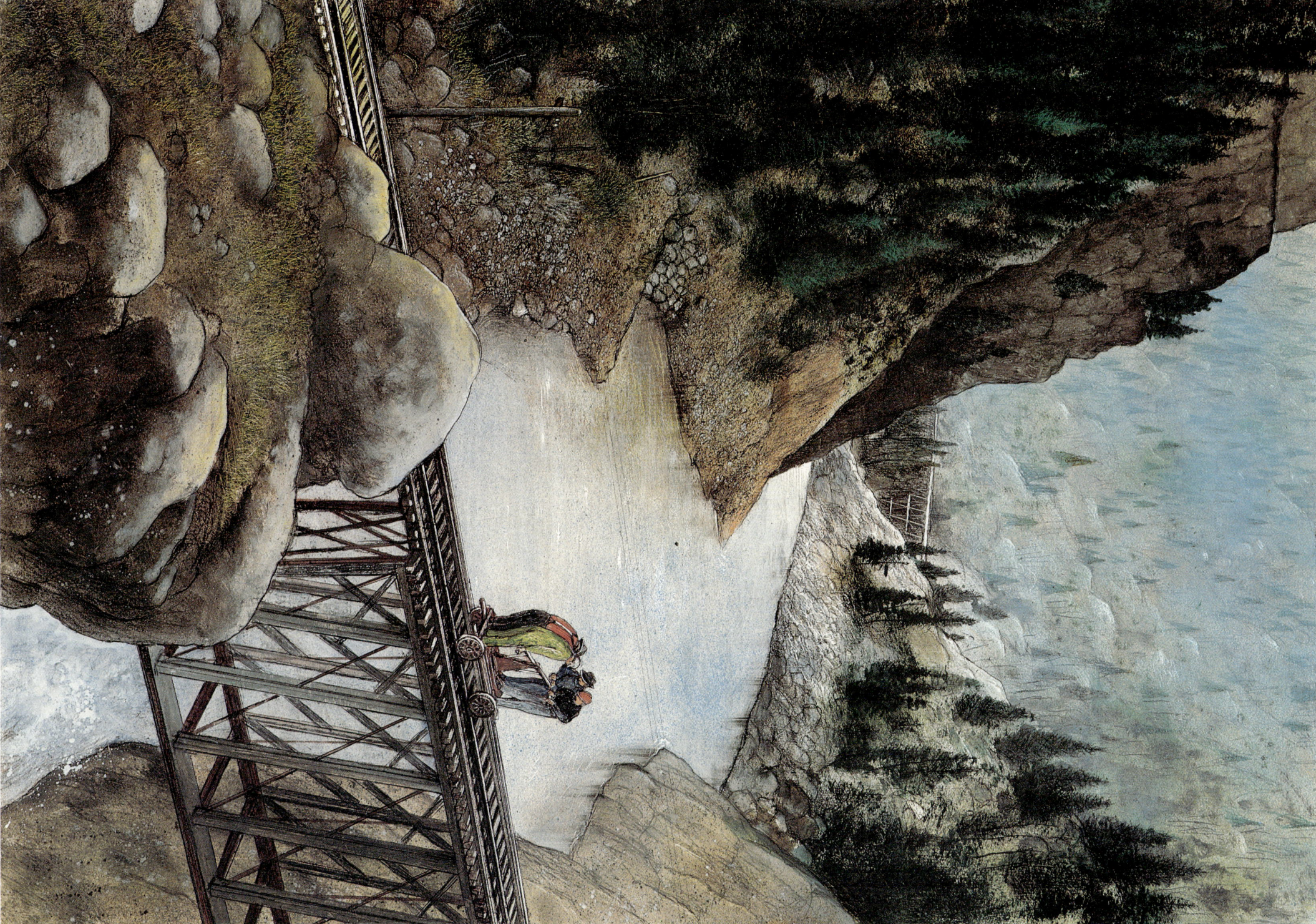

Railway gang in British Columbia

William Kurelek

Part three

With a baby on one's back

Józef Glista, aged 26, and his wife Maria, 22, with a six-month-old son arrived in Canada in June 1929 and travelled across Canada in a closed train till they reached Prince Albert, Saskatchewan. He bought a homestead at Henribourg, put up a sod house that year and, being a carpenter as well as a farmer, built a more permanent home the following year. By 1933 he had 200 acres under cultivation and a large herd of Jersey cows. Unfortunately because of the Depression he could no longer sell his grain. Other calamities destroyed the initial bright prospects. He fell seriously ill while digging a new well in 1934. After he recovered his wife was hospitalized. Their third son Ted, who is today one of my insurance agents and chief promoter of this Polish series, was then a one-year-old baby. With no one else available to care for the child, Józef had to carry him whenever he went into the fields, plowing, disking or cultivating.

One day a horse at the disks bolted and the jerk threw the baby in front of the machine. He'd have been chopped up had the other horse not been placid and stayed put. Józef loved his children and always used to carry Ted on his shoulders even when he didn't have to. The trauma of his near death was such that the father simply unhitched the horses, left the field and never touched it again. The next year he auctioned off the farm, the income of which served only to pay off the taxes, and moved to Toronto.

Despite his adversities, however, Józef was never bitter or resentful. Canada remained his dream, the "Promised Land," if not for himself, certainly for his four sons. W.K.

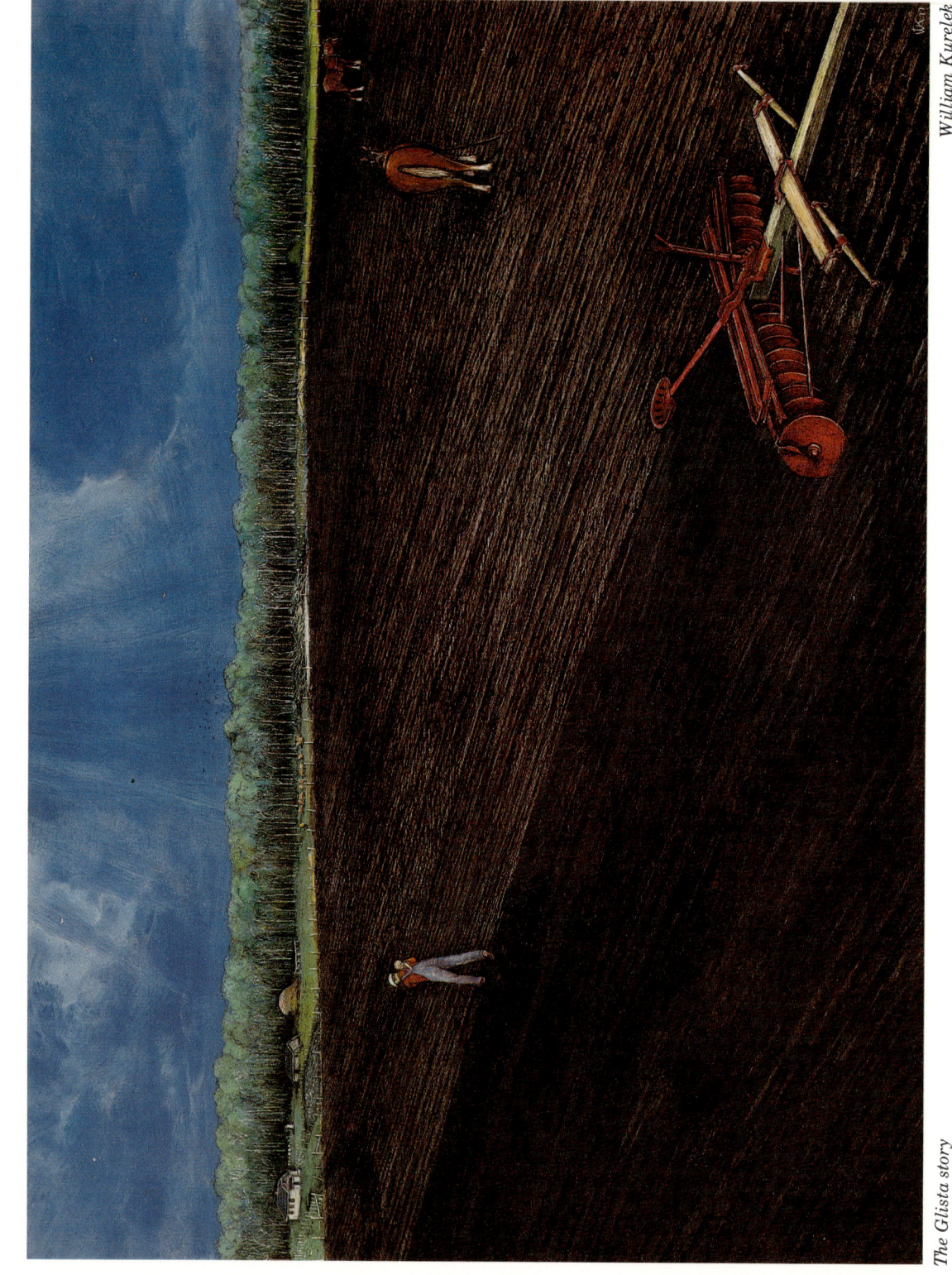

The Glista story
William Kurelek

The hardships they endured

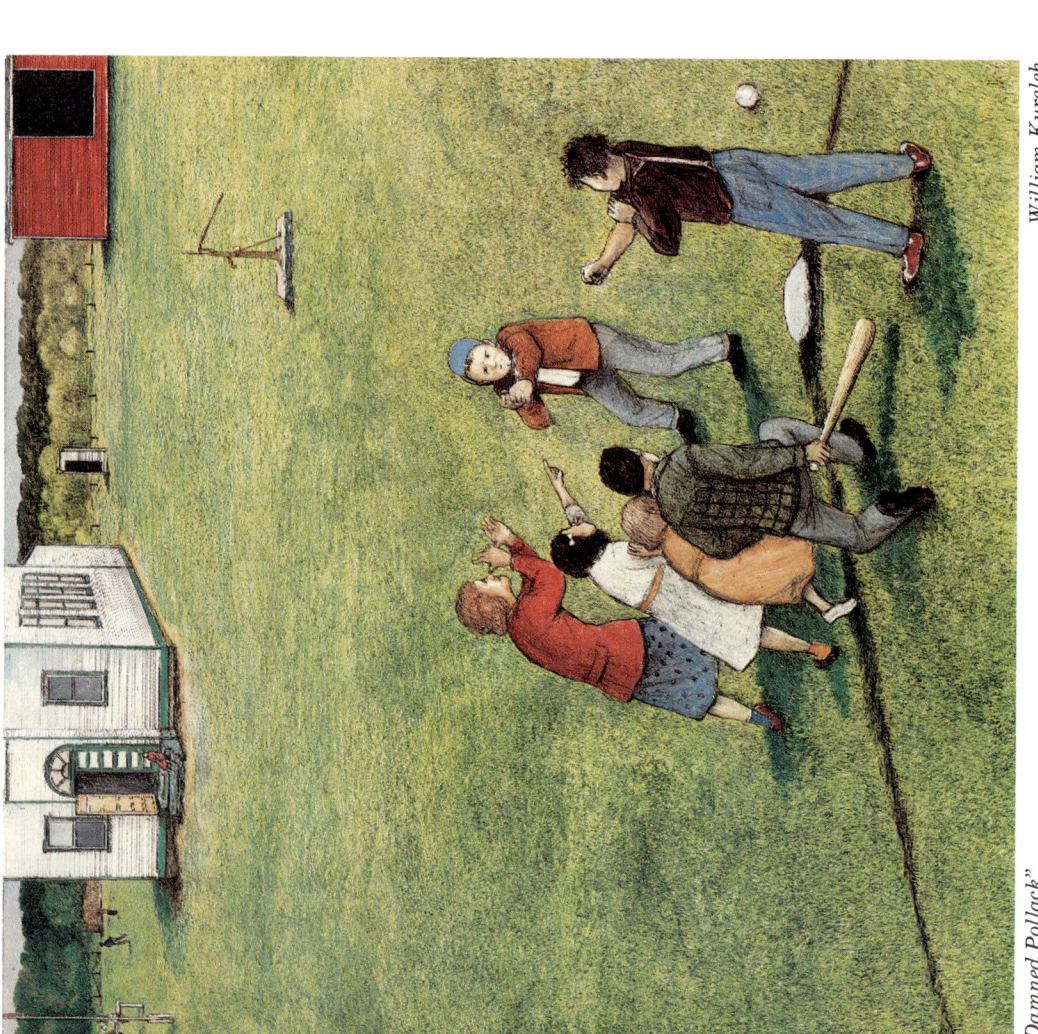

"Damned Pollack" — William Kurelek

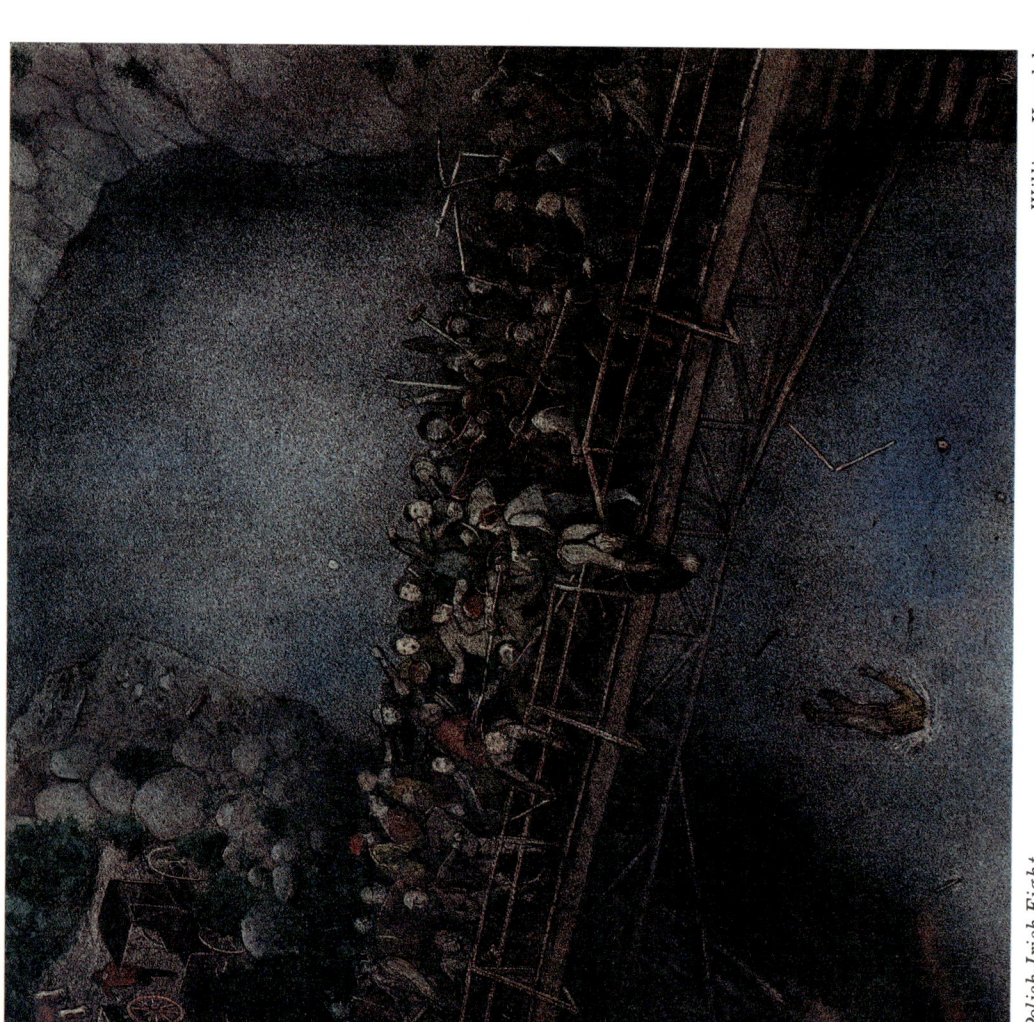

Polish-Irish Fight — William Kurelek

Prejudice *and jealousy*

This picture is the one and only direct reference to my autobiography. The expression "damned Pollack" was part of the name-calling and discriminatory strife that went on in our one-room public school house on the prairies. The central figure in the picture is Joe Gay. Joe was the eldest son of one of three brothers who'd emigrated from Poland in the 30's and settled in the Stonewall district of Manitoba some two miles from my father's farm. Their real name was Gayski but they shortened it to Gay. When Joe appeared at Victoria School he couldn't speak a word of English. My brother John and I, who'd gone through the same trauma of isolation two years before, befriended him early and we became fast friends.

We chummed not only at school but whenever our parents freed us from chores after school or on weekends. Our bicycles enabled us to explore the countryside for miles in all directions. Sometimes we even got into trouble as when we raided old Shewchuk's garden and were chased by him. What I appreciated most, even to this day, is that we were able to commune together with nature.

But there must have been some fellow Slav feeling between us — this came out especially when we were persecuted by the school WASP group. I recall Joe had some such racist experience one day as I've depicted in this picture. Name-calling and fists were the two main weapons. John and I had a fight with the same group a few days later before the air was cleared and Slavs and British made up. Historian Makowski makes frequent reference to early prejudice against Poles in Canada. Most of that is gone now. Perhaps the Polish jokes we used to hear a few years ago were faint survivals of it. W.K.

One of the difficulties for Polish settlers in the Renfrew district of Ontario was Polish-Irish antagonism. According to historian Makowski, analyzing the rivalry now is difficult. He suggests the Irish fault was jealousy of Polish industriousness and prosperity and the Poles' fault was their refusal to socialize with non-Poles. Even today parish records in Wilno and Barry's Bay show only 3% of marriages are mixed.

During an election at the turn of the century, there was a regular war between the Polish and Irish elements. The Polish version of it is that the Irish planned to come to Barry's Bay and beat up any Pole refusing to vote for the English candidate. The Poles gathered to prevent their coming and the two forces met at a bridge.

It's not known who won except that in the course of the battle the combatants destroyed the bridge. Eventually the two nationalities did learn to live in harmony — the more so since they shared the same Catholic faith. W.K.

Note: According to Makowski, the battle lasted three days. Kurelek pictured it as taking place at night. Ed.

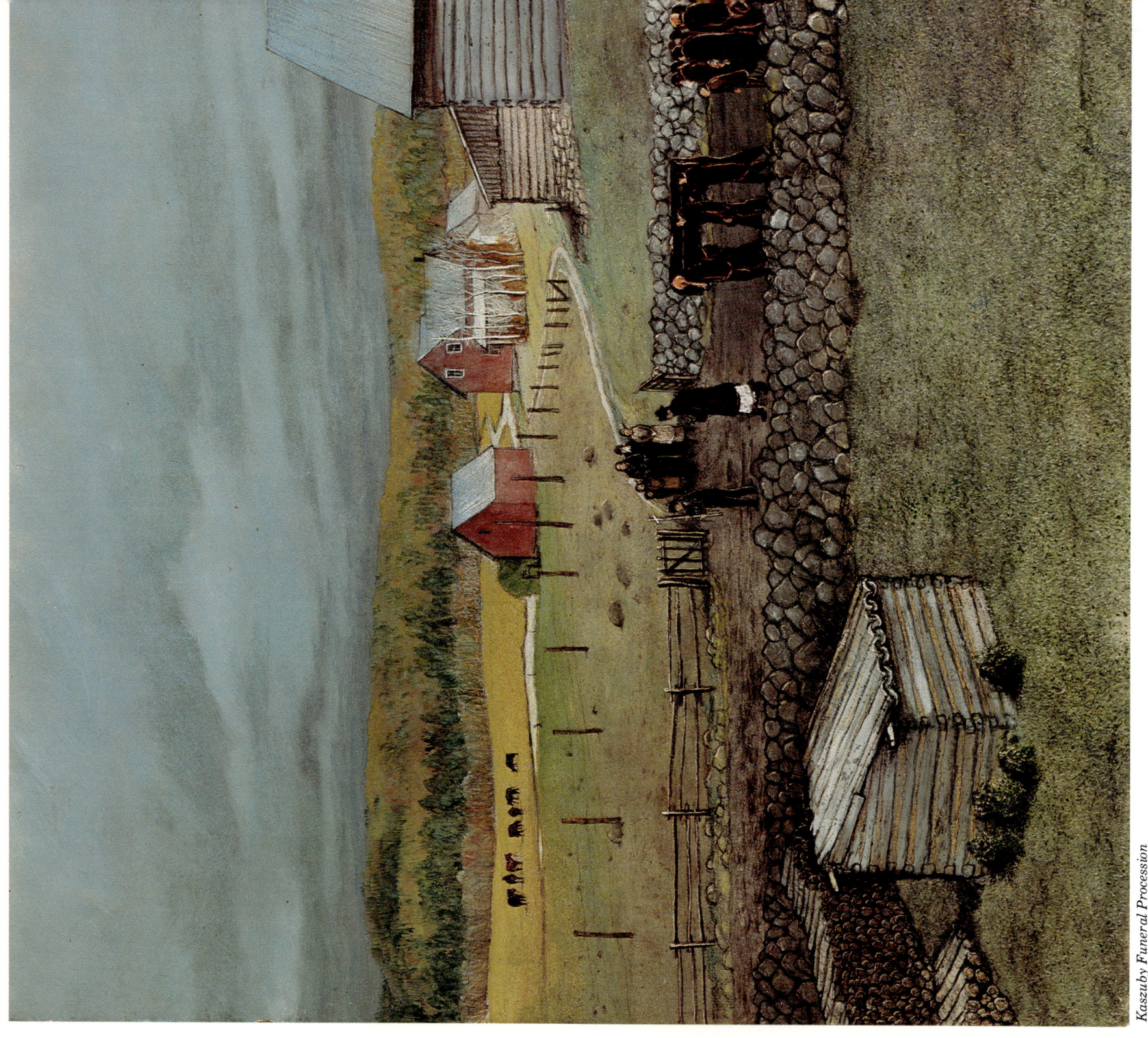

Kaszuby Funeral Procession

In a coffin of birchbark

I've chosen a gray, fall day for this picture, to match the sadness of the occasion. Martin Racoski's farm is the setting. In the panel of the frame I've put in photographs of the gravestones at the Wilno church cemetery. The names on the stones are supposed to get across the Polishness of the scene. But I'm not sure that even with "antiquing" I've managed to tone down the starkness of the photo.

The coffins of the first pioneers were no more than birchbark woven over two poles. On this primitive stretcher the body was placed, wrapped in a white sheet. Polish religious customs to do with death survived immigration, however, and at the very least neighbors would gather at the home of the deceased

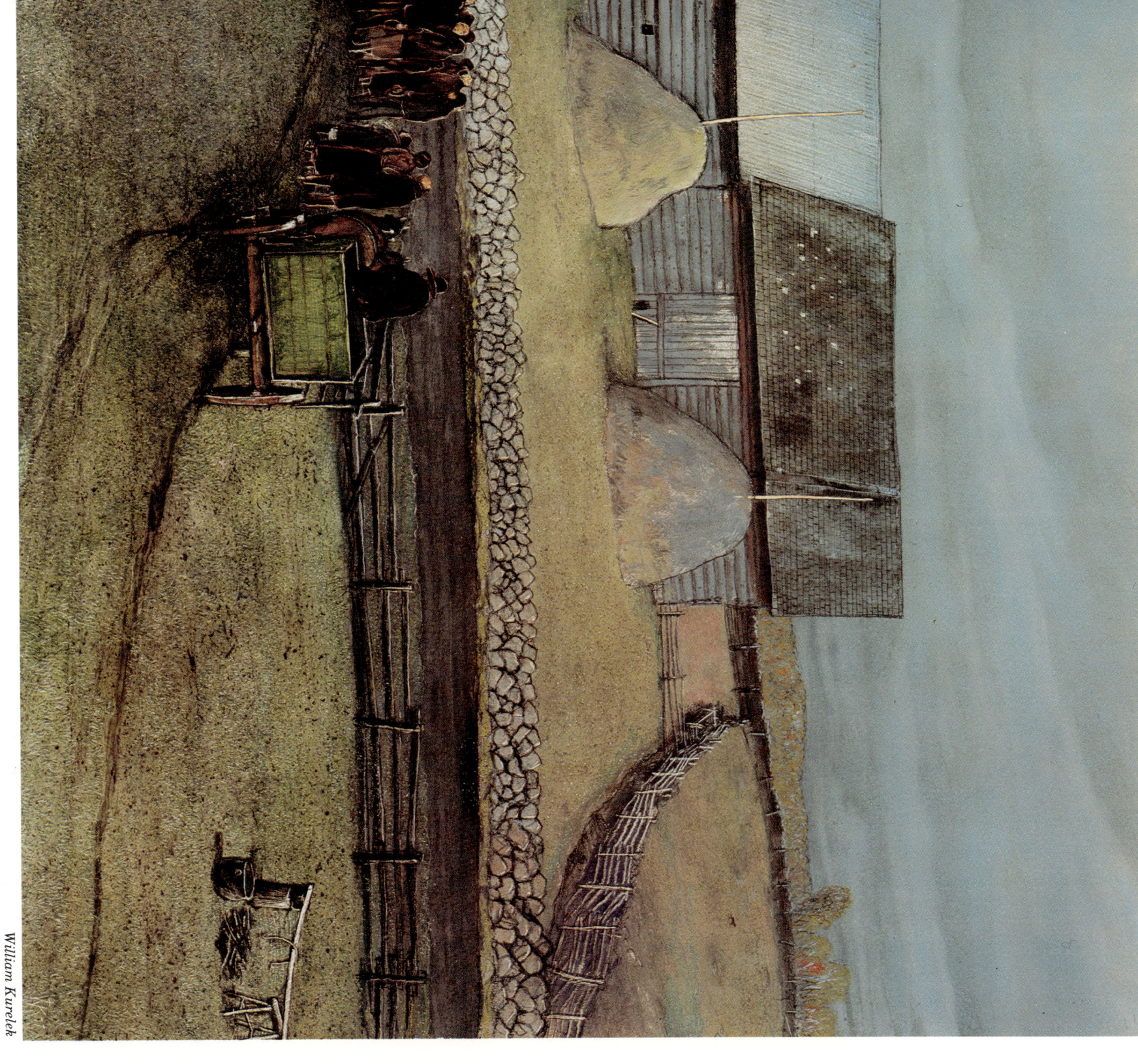

the night before the burial to say the rosary. The procession the following day to the farm burial plot (church cemeteries came later) rather resembled the Old Country one. At the head was the boy carrying a large cross. Then came the priest carrying a crucifix and a breviary and wearing a biretta and white stole (I have him with a coat over top because the autumn winds are chilly). Next came a boy carrying holy water to sprinkle the grave with (I've left him out). Then, six male friends or relatives came carrying the coffin on their shoulders followed by the immediate family of the deceased, friends and neighbors. The procession ended with a horse and wagon in case someone should faint along the way. Neighbors waited with bare heads at their gates to join the procession. W.K.

William Kurelek

Part four

In the service of God

This simple but saintly man was born of peasant stock and grew up to be an apprentice in blacksmithing in both Poland and Germany. To his father's disappointment, however, during the course of his training he decided to enter the religious community, known as The Missionary Oblates of Mary Immaculate, as a Brother. After taking his vows in Holland he asked for foreign service and that was how in 1896 he found himself at the Lac La Biche mission north of Edmonton, Alberta. His hard work, initiative, prayers and humility made him indispensable to the mission station.

When his arm was cut up in a sawmill he dismissed the accident simply with the words: "It's God's will." Actually it was six painful days before they managed to get him to Edmonton to have it amputated. The Cree Indians around the mission had a special respect for him. Having lost the buffalo as a source of food they were sometimes near starvation. Brother Anthony got permission from the Church authorities to raise a herd of 200 pigs which practically fed the tribe.

Brother Anthony spent 37 years at the service of students at Collège Saint-Jean (St. John's College) in Edmonton, where he died in 1947. The process for his beatification is well under way. W.K.

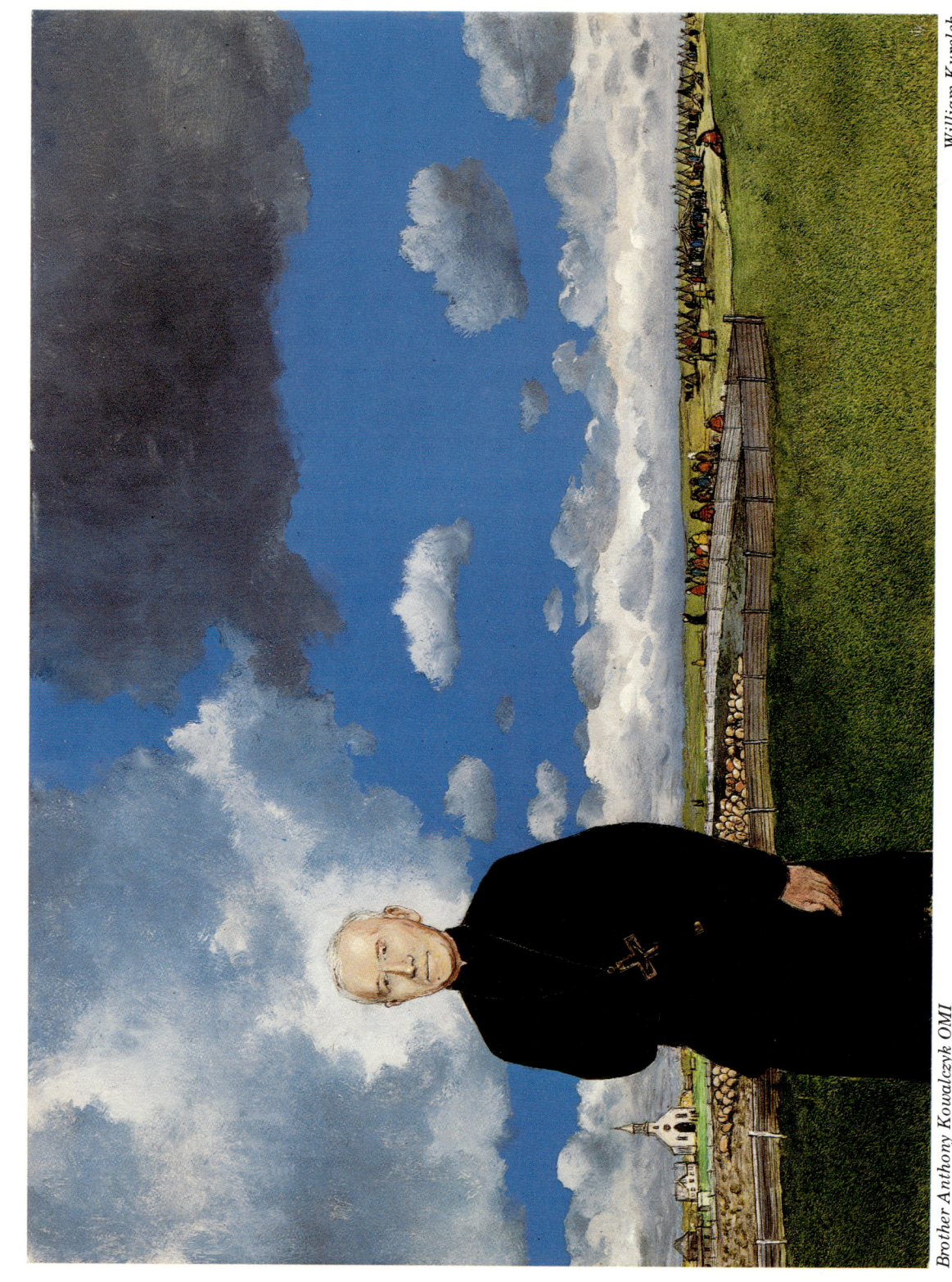

Brother Anthony Kowalczyk OMI *William Kurelek*

The courage they showed

Valor of the highest order

The Poles are well known for fighting qualities like the courage and chivalry for which Flight Lieutenant Andrew Charles Mynarski won the Victoria Cross in the last war.

Born in Winnipeg, he joined the Royal Canadian Air Force in 1940 at the age of 23. During a bombing mission over France a week after D-day, the Lancaster bomber where he was mid-upper gunner was hit by an enemy fighter and burst into flames. The crew was ordered to bale out. Mynarski, because of his position, had the first chance to jump. But, just before he did so, he noticed that the tail gunner was trapped in his turret by damaged hydraulics.

According to the official citation, "without hesitation, Pilot Officer Mynarski made his way through the flames in an endeavor to reach the rear turret and release the gunner. Whilst so doing his parachute and his clothing, up to the waist, were set on fire. All his efforts to move the turret and free the gunner were in vain. Eventually the rear gunner clearly indicated to him that there was nothing more he could do and that he should try to save his own life. Pilot Officer Mynarski reluctantly went back through the flames to the escape hatch. There, as a last gesture to the trapped gunner, he turned toward him, stood to attention in his flaming clothing and saluted, before he jumped out of the aircraft.

"Pilot Officer Mynarski's descent was seen by French people on the ground. Both his parachute and clothing were on fire. He was found eventually by the French, but was so severely burnt that he died from his injuries."

Miraculously, the rear gunner who Mynarski had tried so unsuccessfully to save, actually escaped when the aircraft crashed and it was he who later testified to Mynarski's gallantry.

The citation concluded: "Pilot Officer Mynarski lost his life by a most conspicuous act of heroism which called for valor of the highest order." The Victoria Cross awarded him was only the second given in R.C.A.F. history.

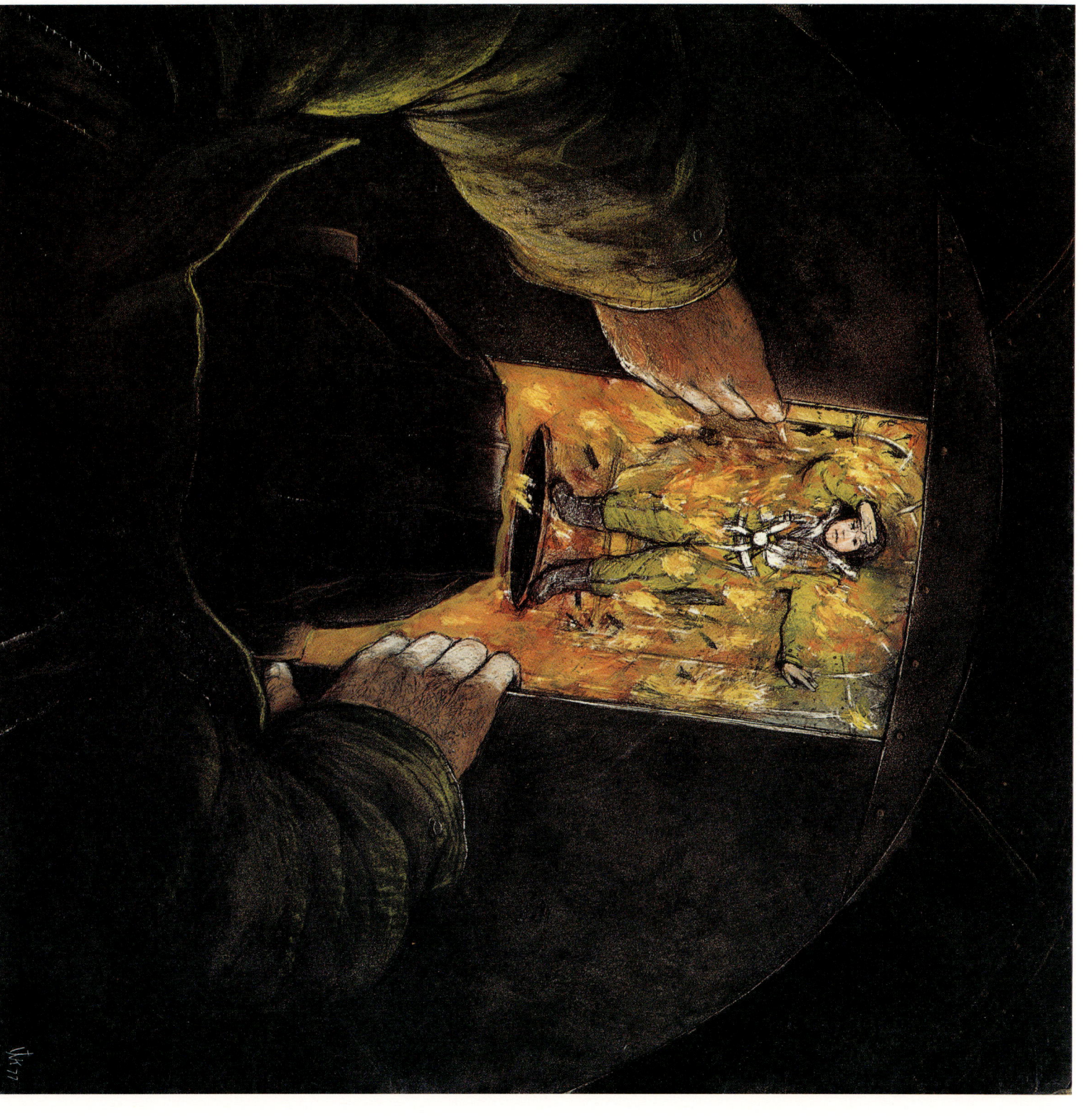

The courage of Andrew Mynarski — William Kurelek

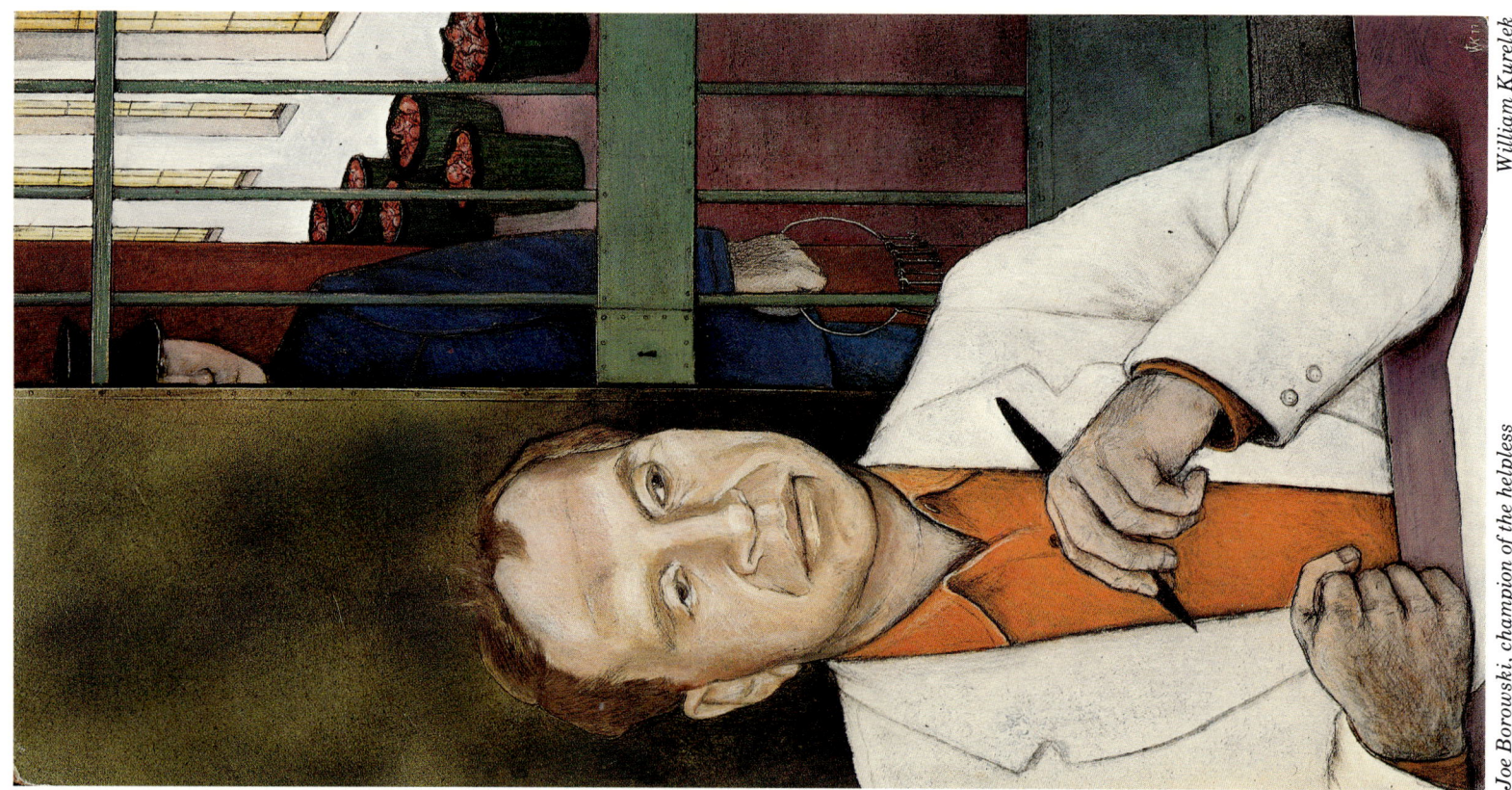

Joe Borowski, champion of the helpless   *William Kurelek*

Fighting for principles

Whether people agree or not with his choice of language or his methods of protest, many, myself included, truly admire Joe Borowski for standing up for his principles. When the NDP party swept into power in Manitoba in 1969 the new premier Ed Schreyer (now Canada's Governor-General) appointed many so-called "ethnics" to his cabinet. The Minister of Transport was Joe Borowski, MLA for Thompson. He proved to be a boat-rocking source of embarrassment, even to his party, on several moral issues. Some of these issues were drugs, Indians, censorship and abortions. Eventually he resigned from the party over these issues and even went to jail rather than pay taxes to a government that used taxpayers' money to kill unborn children. I have represented him here symbolically, as a persecuted fighter voicing protest.

An article by Winnipeg lawyer Chris Lorenc summed up Joe Borowski thus: "... Joe Borowski means well in whatever stand he takes. Some people claim that he is a religious fanatic out to seek personal glory. I say that Joe Borowski is a man of principle, an honest politician, a man who is probably one of the most intelligent MLA's in the Legislature. He is not afraid to say what he feels and while doing so doesn't mean to injure innocent people. It's the politicians, the opportunists who strive to walk over Joe for their own ends. He has a firm belief in democracy, believing that this system tops any other in the world. Freedom of speech, of expression is very important to him, to you and me. After all, isn't that what democracy is all about? . . ." W.K.

Note: As this book goes to the printer in the summer of 1981, Mr. Borowski is midway through a 90-day fast to protest that the unborn are not protected in the Charter of Human Rights proposed for Canada's constitution. Ed.

31

Part five

Bringing news from home

Like other nationalities the Poles tended to stick to their own kind for companionship when they arrived in Canada. They didn't know the English language or that of any other immigrant group when they first arrived. Here we have a group crowded together in a bedroom listening to tales of a newly arrived immigrant about the situation back in Poland.

In the bigger cities like Toronto there were unscrupulous landlords who took advantage of that clanishness to put up large rambling boardinghouses near the waterfront and cater to each group separately, be they Bulgarians, Poles, Macedonians or Ukrainians. The men's rooms were mere cubicles, the food the plainest and the conveniences the most primitive. But no immigrant squealed to the city authorities about these conditions. He preferred the cheap lodging simply because he was trying to save as much money as possible from his laboring job to send back to his family in Poland or to buy a house or farm over here before bringing his family over. W.K.

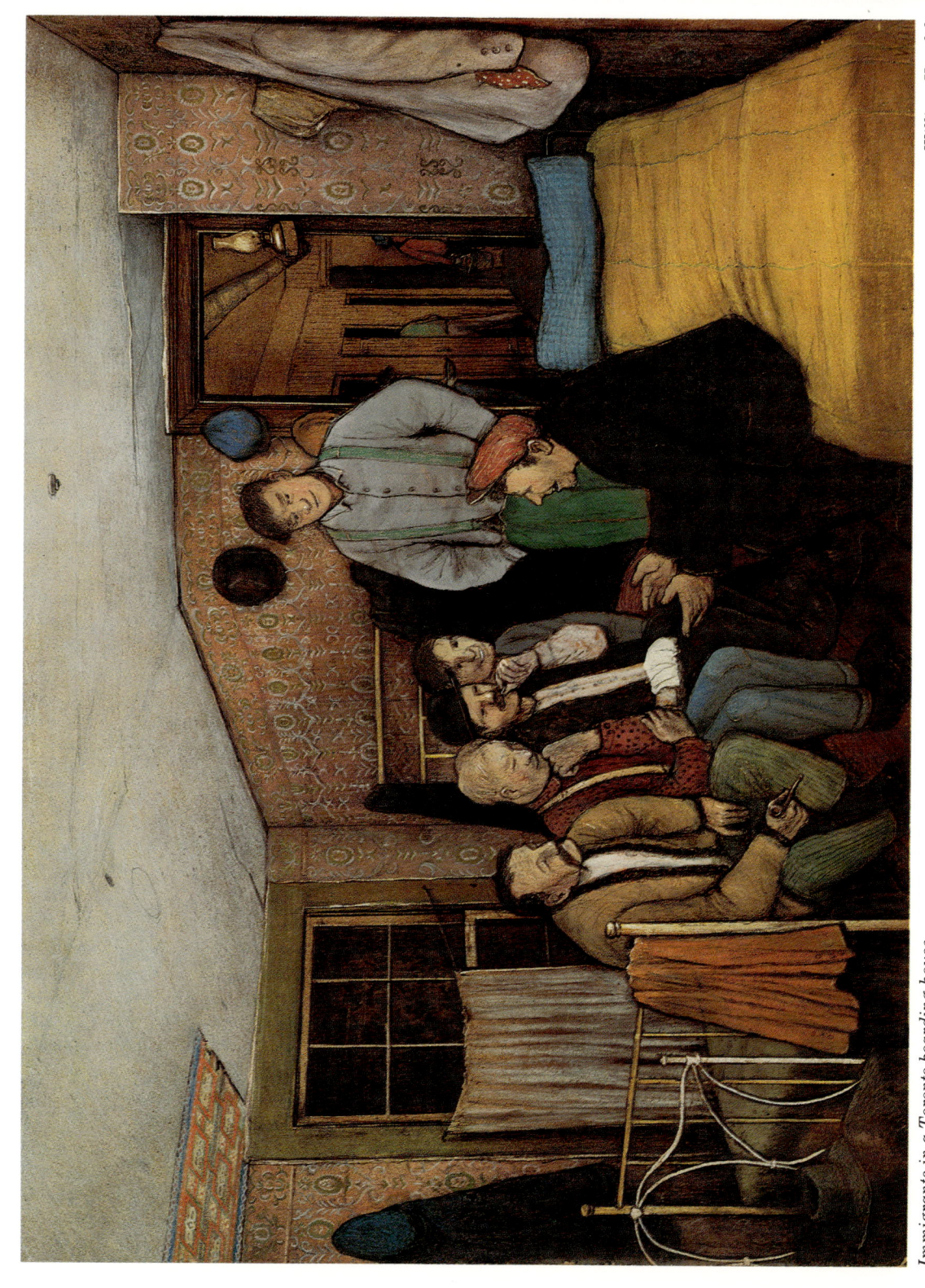

Immigrants in a Toronto boarding house

William Kurelek

The joys they shared

The Irish priest who learned Polish

When I was doing research on Ukrainian settlement in Canada, I discovered to my surprise that there was a sizable community of our people right in the heart of the Maritimes, in Scottish Cape Breton Island. I therefore stayed in Sydney, Nova Scotia, for a few weeks to get acquainted with them and the Maritimes in general. It was winter and the skies were often depressingly overcast. The smoke of the foundries and the steel mills added to the pall as in this picture.

Apart from the Kaszuby settlement, Poles and Ukrainians tend to be found near each other in Canada. And sure enough when I began research on this series I found there were Poles in Sydney too. The first group consisting of four families arrived there back in 1901.

Eventually their community grew to a population of one and a half thousand, enough to form a Catholic parish, St. Mary's of the Nativity. They managed to find Polish priests at first, but when finally in 1920 ran short of them, an energetic Irishman, Father Leo O'Connell, took over, first as assistant, then, in 1929, as parish priest. He served them in that capacity for 40 years, showing sincere devotion to their welfare. They loved him in return, all the more because he had made himself one of them by learning to speak fluent Polish.

I've depicted him chatting to parishioners on the street as a work shift comes out of the steel mills. W.K.

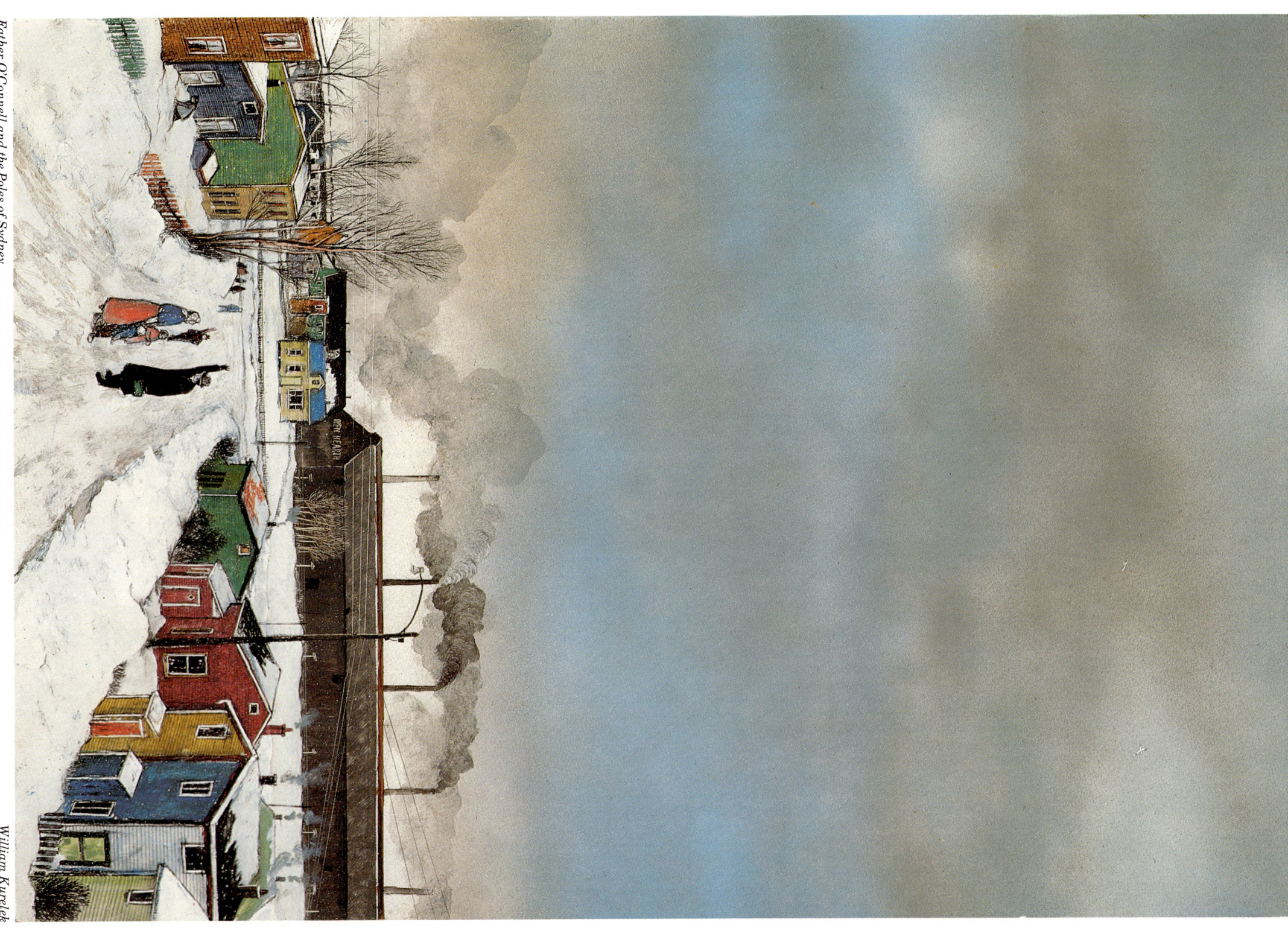

Father O'Connell and the Poles of Sydney

William Kurelek

The twelve dishes of Christmas

I've set this Christmas Eve feast at Otter Lake because it's in Quebec and some recognition must be given to Poles living in that province. Otter Lake is on the north side of the Ottawa River between Pembroke and Hull. I set the time of this picture back in the 1920's hoping thereby to assume Polish Christmas customs of the Old Country would be in fact substantially preserved, since Ukrainian Christmas customs were mostly intact in our own home in the West back in the 30's. But the Kaszuby Poles to whom I showed the painting just after it was finished hardly recognized anything in it. I therefore had to assume that the granny in the picture, fresh from Poland on her children's invitation, had inspired them to revive some Old Country culture. That's her wagging her finger at her grandson impatient to get eating and reaching for an extra *oplatek*.

The Old Country feast is preceded by a few formalities. Grace, which is said standing up, has to wait for the appearance of the first star in the sky. This is followed by the ceremonial sharing of the *oplatek*, a thin unleavened wafer stamped with the figures of the God Child, the Blessed Mary and the Holy Angels. It is known as the "bread of love." A plate full of these wafers is set in the middle of the table where we Ukrainians place the three-tiered *kolach*. The bundle of wafers is tied with a ribbon and sprig of evergreen and laid on an embroidered cloth on some hay in a plate after being fetched from church where enough wafers have been blessed for the whole community. The wife starts the ceremony by offering her husband the first *oplatek*. They break it, eat and embrace and kiss. Then the rest around the table do the same. This is followed by a toast of *krupnik* (alcohol and honey) from a decanter (children use fruit juice). Only then can they dig into the twelve main dishes (representing the twelve apostles) and they do so with gusto having observed an Advent fast beforehand.

Roughly the order of dishes as the family would eat them is: *barszcz* (beet soup); *uszka* (dumplings with mushrooms); jellied fish; *golabki* (cabbage rolls stuffed with rice or buckwheat); fried carp; *pierogi* (dumplings stuffed with cabbage, cheese or potatoes); fruit compote; varied baked sweets (apple strudel, poppy-seed rolls).

You may notice two empty chairs. They are ceremonially put there to welcome unexpected guests. Unlike Ukrainians, Poles always have a Christmas tree even if they are so poor that they have to use colored paper to make decorations. Two candles, one at each end of the table, are tied with blue ribbons and hay under the tablecloth symbolizes Christ's birth in a manger. A sheaf of wheat stands on the floor near a window and after the supper it's used to tie straw bands round the fruit trees in the belief of a better crop the following summer. Of course in Canada's cold North and West, Polish settlers found hardly any fruit trees would grow anyway. Another doubtful survival in Canada was the custom, on Christmas Eve, of giving farm animals an extra portion of feed, with wafers mixed in. W.K.

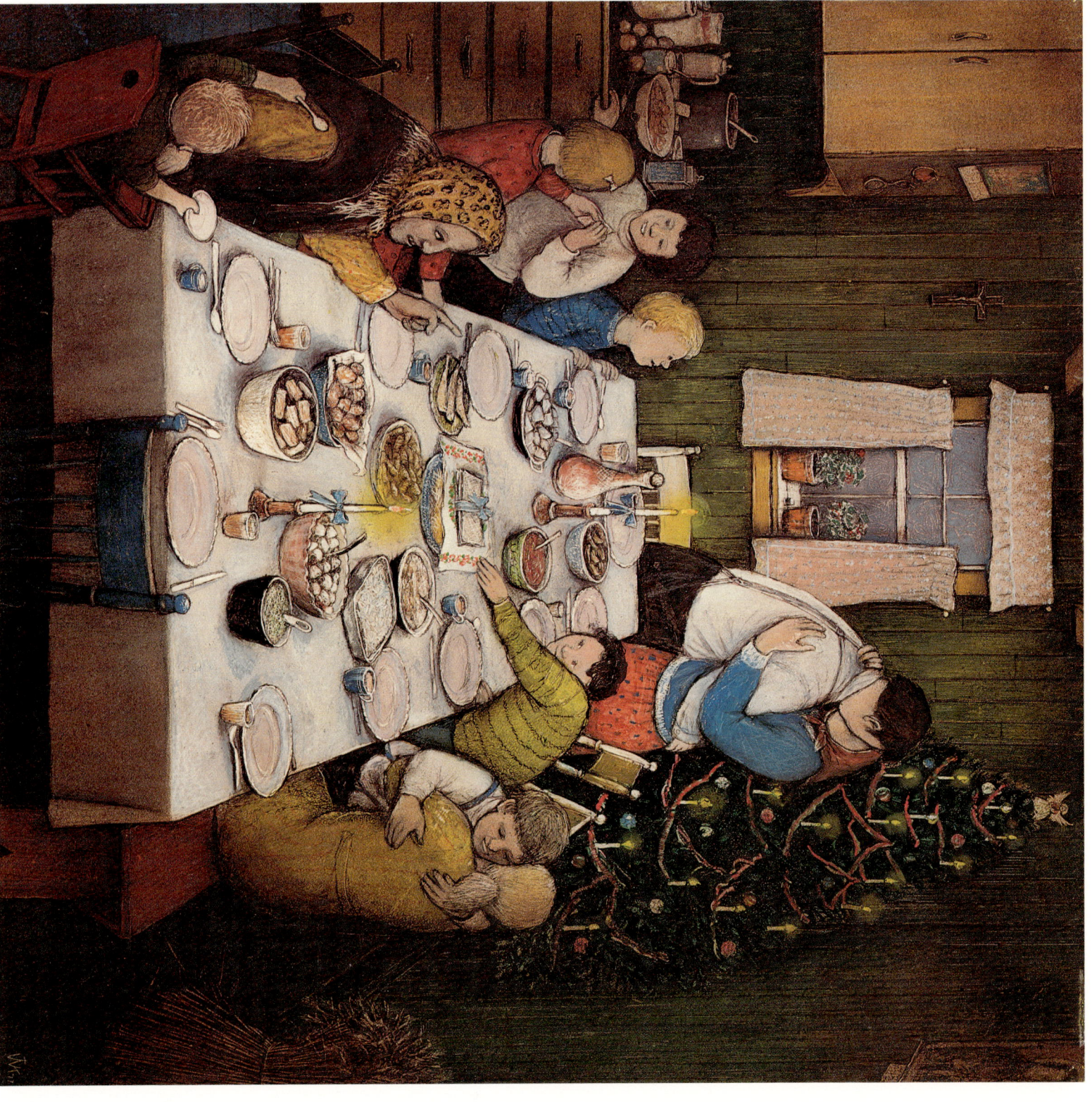

Christmas at Otter Lake, Quebec

William Kurelek

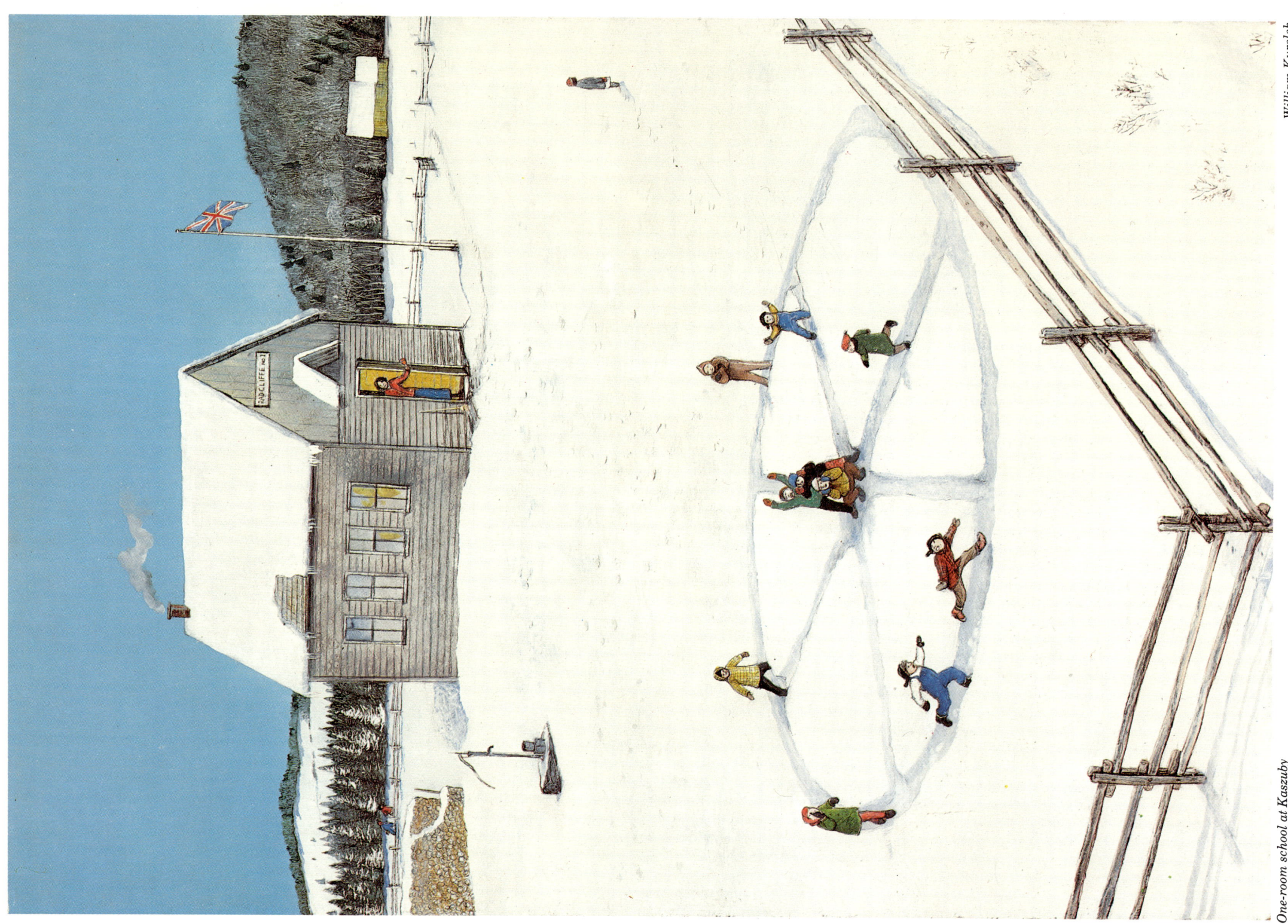

One-room school at Kaszuby William Kurelek

After the first snow

Roman showed me this school across the road from the Kosnaski store on Long Lake. It has now been made over into a private house since the pupils are bused into Combermere. I used my own memory of attending a one room schoolhouse on the prairies and my imagination to reconstruct the original appearance of Radcliffe No. 1 Public School. Later that day we visited the Lehovitch farm which I used as a model for the wedding picture. Mrs. Lehovitch was able to add some details on school life in the 30's and 40's when she was a pupil at Radcliffe No. 1. I based this painting on one of her memories.

The school was built in 1917. Before that, children of the neighborhood simply didn't go to school. The teacher in Mrs. Lehovitch's school days, although of French Canadian origin, taught in English. She must have had a hard time as most of the children spoke only Polish at first. Going to school wasn't easy for the children either. Once for example they were scared by a bear which was eating a sheep on a farm near the school. In winter, if snowfall was heavy, they'd have to wade through drifts as high as their waists. But they enjoyed the company of fellow students when they got to school by playing various old games, some of which I remember, such as Fox and Geese (shown here), Hippey-Tippey, Hop-Scotch, Red Rover, London Bridge, and *Lapanka*, a Polish tag game. W.K.

A wedding lasted days

I have done several similar paintings on Ukrainian weddings. I consulted Frank Ritza for this one because he used to play the violin at weddings and dances. He told me of one Old Country custom, that of the *druzba*, still practiced in the 20's and 30's. The *druzba* is a man chosen by the wedding party to drive around the district in a buggy festooned with ribbons to invite people to the wedding. On arrival at a farmhouse he'd fire a revolver three times into the air. Wearing white gloves and carrying a cane he would then chant a customary form of invitation at the door.

On the wedding day itself one of the two fiddlers at the ball didn't go to the church ceremony but went directly to the bride's home where he positioned himself at the gate. He would play the traditional wedding welcome tune for each family as it arrived, and some, out of appreciation, would drop a quarter into his violin.

Some people used to come to the weddings with ribbons and pompons decorating their buggies, wagons and horses. But I was not sure what those looked like, so I left them out. Frank pointed out that the Kaszubs were so deculturalized under the Prussians that they accepted a completely Canadian dress when they arrived here. For the bride and groom accordingly, the outfit was probably something ordered from an Eaton's catalogue. The setting here is Lehovitch's farm for despite its stoniness it makes a charming composition. The idea of dancing on an outdoor platform built for the big day, and feasting and drinking beside the house may well hark back to the Old Country, village square celebrations. These were traditionally gay times except that when the wedding lasted three days, Old Country style, it might end with a fight. W.K.

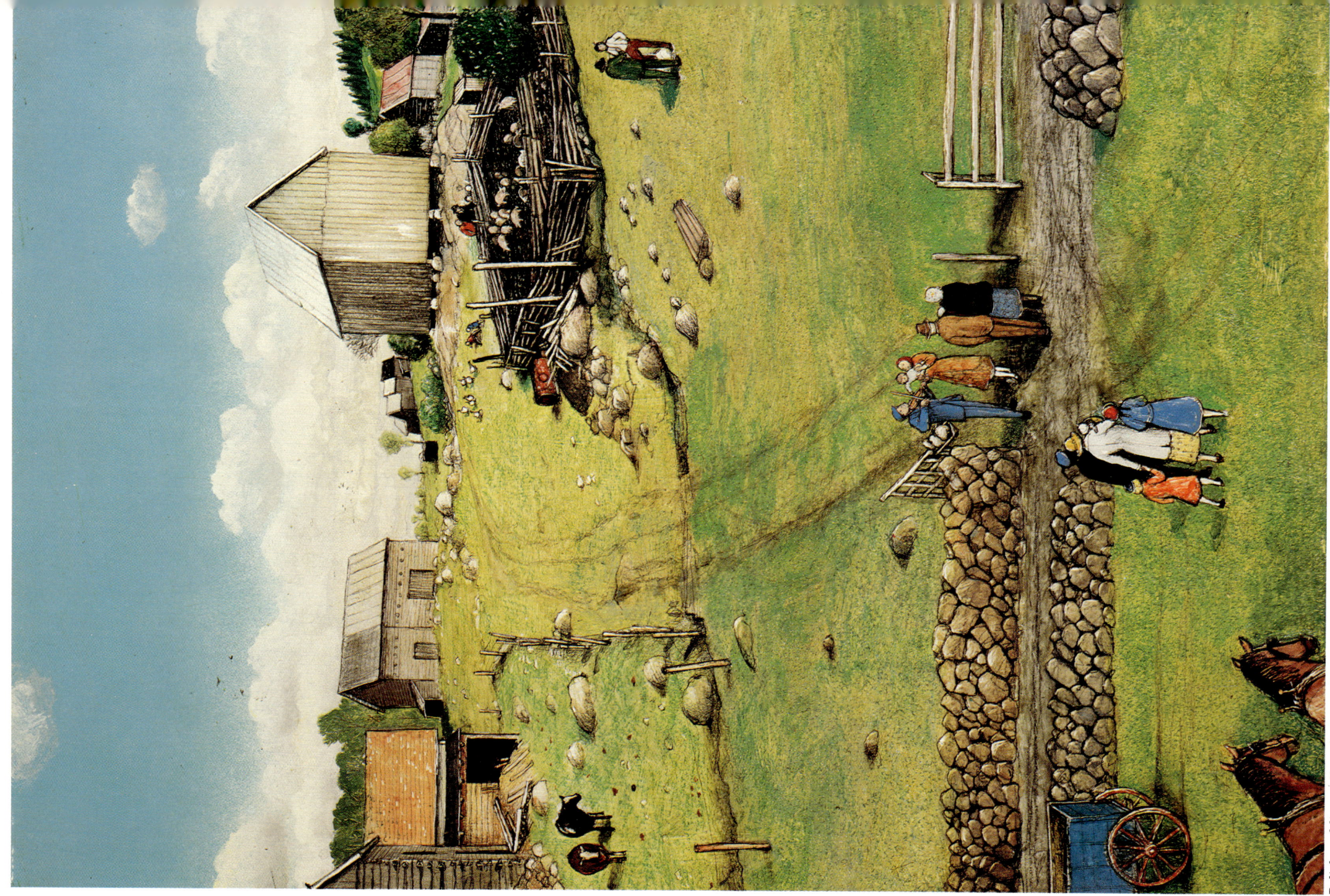

Polish wedding at Kaszuby

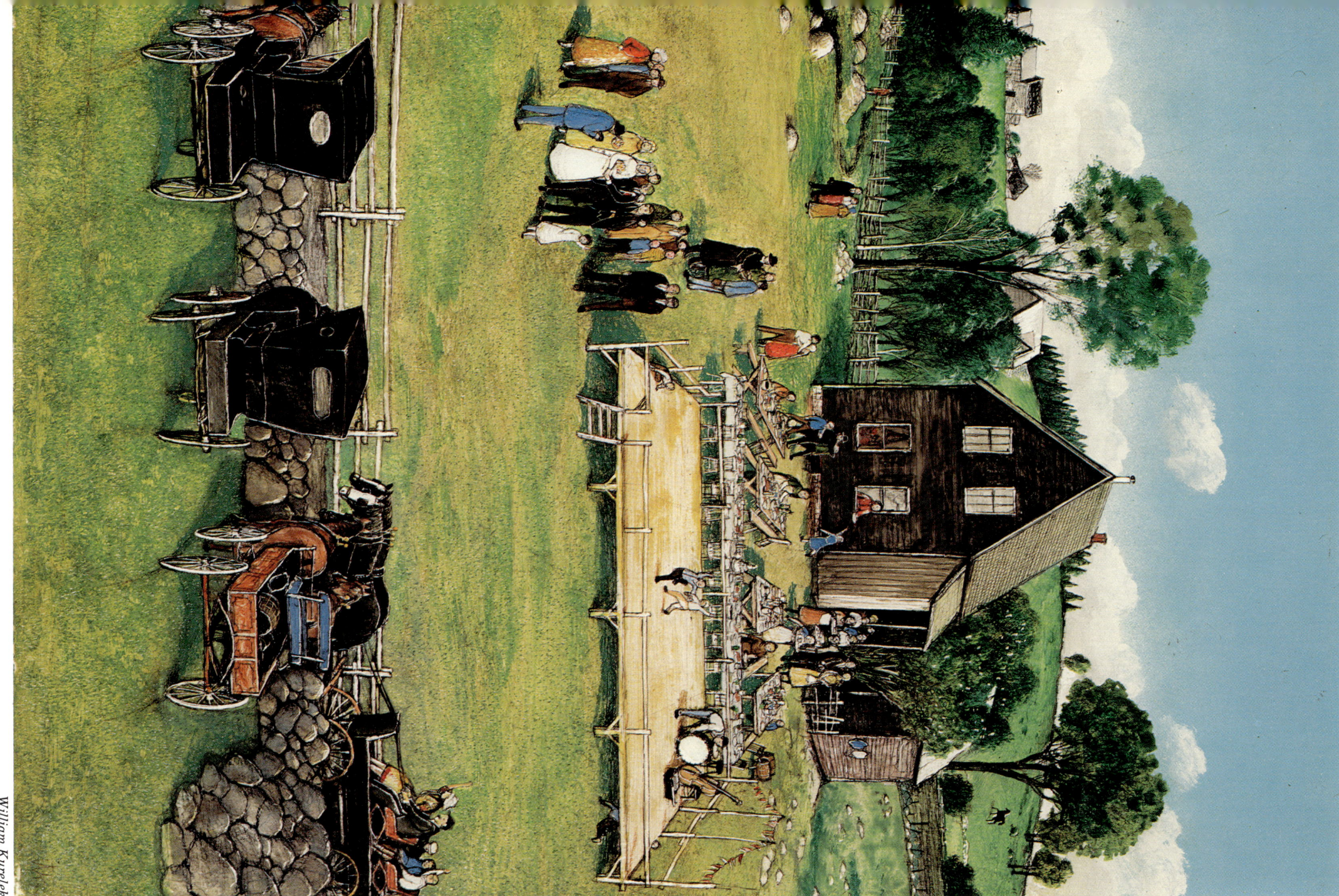

William Kurelek

Part six

On the night run

Our second nearest neighbors at Combermere are the Yantha family — Alex, Theresa and five children. Alex drives a big lumber truck out of Barry's Bay each weekend on the night run, mostly into Toronto or Montreal. A trucker's life is a lonely, sometimes dangerous one. Here we see Alex on the 401 somewhere between Belleville and Montreal plunging through the rain with two trailers in tow. For relaxation Alex loves hunting and playing the accordion. I chose him to represent yet another responsible job or profession that Poles are into nowadays in Canada.

Theresa checks on my farmhouse and studio when we are away in the city, to see if the heat is on and the basement isn't flooding. Her youngest boy, Danny, plays with our boys when they are out there and the older one, Richard, cuts our grass, weeds the garden and does other farm chores. We appreciate them as neighbors. W.K.

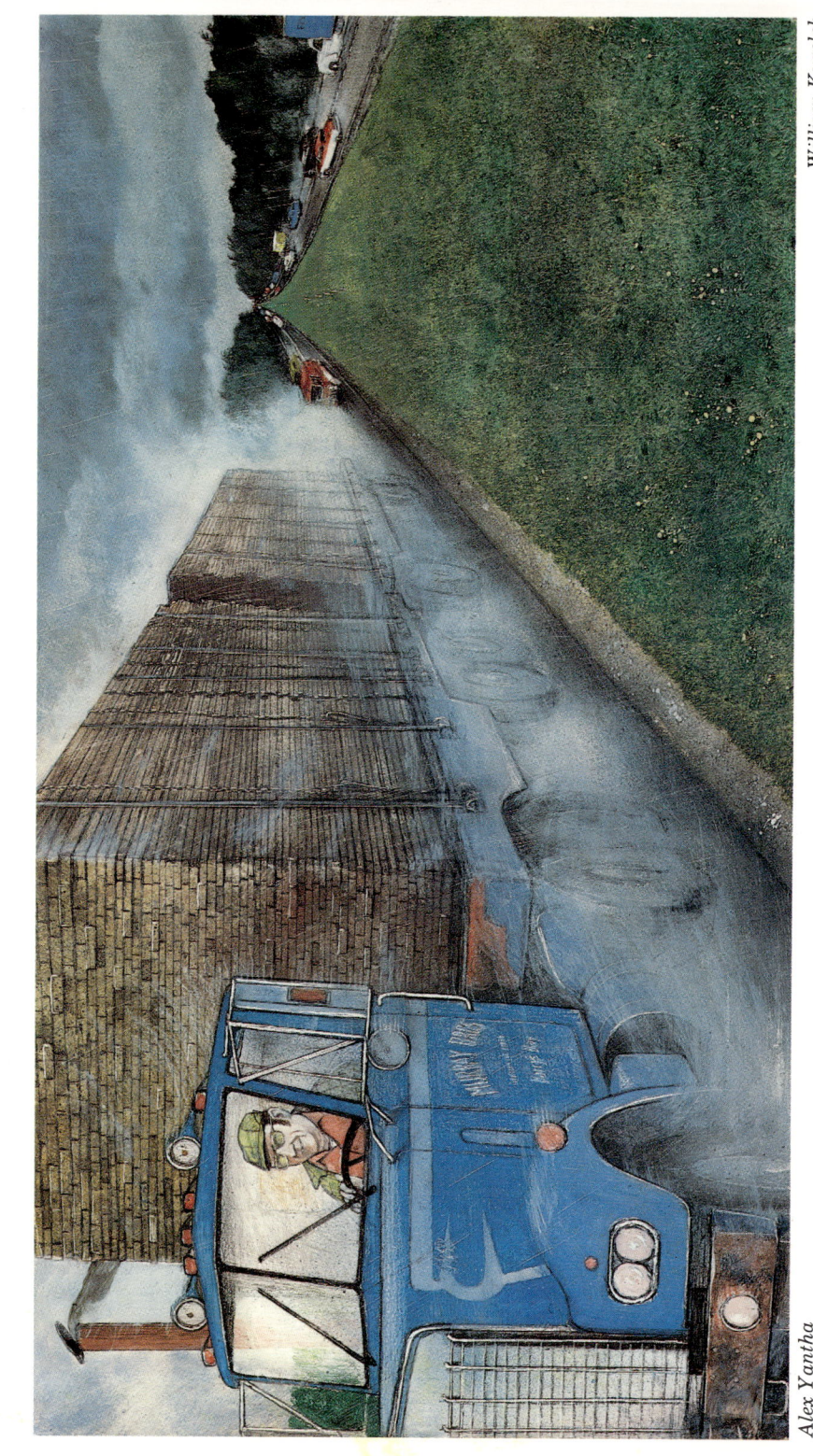

Alex Yantha
William Kurelek

Friends and neighbors

In the village market

In the village of Combermere, Ontario, the post office and my farm studio are situated at the edge of the Kaszuby Polish settlement. Over half the village is Polish. In such small towns, the men often have two or even three jobs. Ernie Peplinski, the affable owner of Valley Market, one of Combermere's two grocery stores, is also on call as one of the six firemen on the town's fire brigade. I've represented him here serving a young customer at his meat counter. At the time I did this painting he had also just been newly elected councillor of the municipality. His wife Nancy works in the store and often part-time helpers come in.

There is an amusing story that goes with my featuring the meat counter in this painting. I was, as usual, on a three-week total fast while on a painting trip. Normally, at such a time, I avoid the sight of tempting foods. But here, in order to get across the idea of North American affluence in which Polish Canadians share, I had to display the variety of meats we can buy. I asked Ernie for a hefty slice of everything in his showcase. Imagine the torture of having those finely spiced aromas wafting into my nostrils as I arranged them on my painting table and proceeded to use them as models. I ate them all with great relish a few days later when my fast officially ended. W.K.

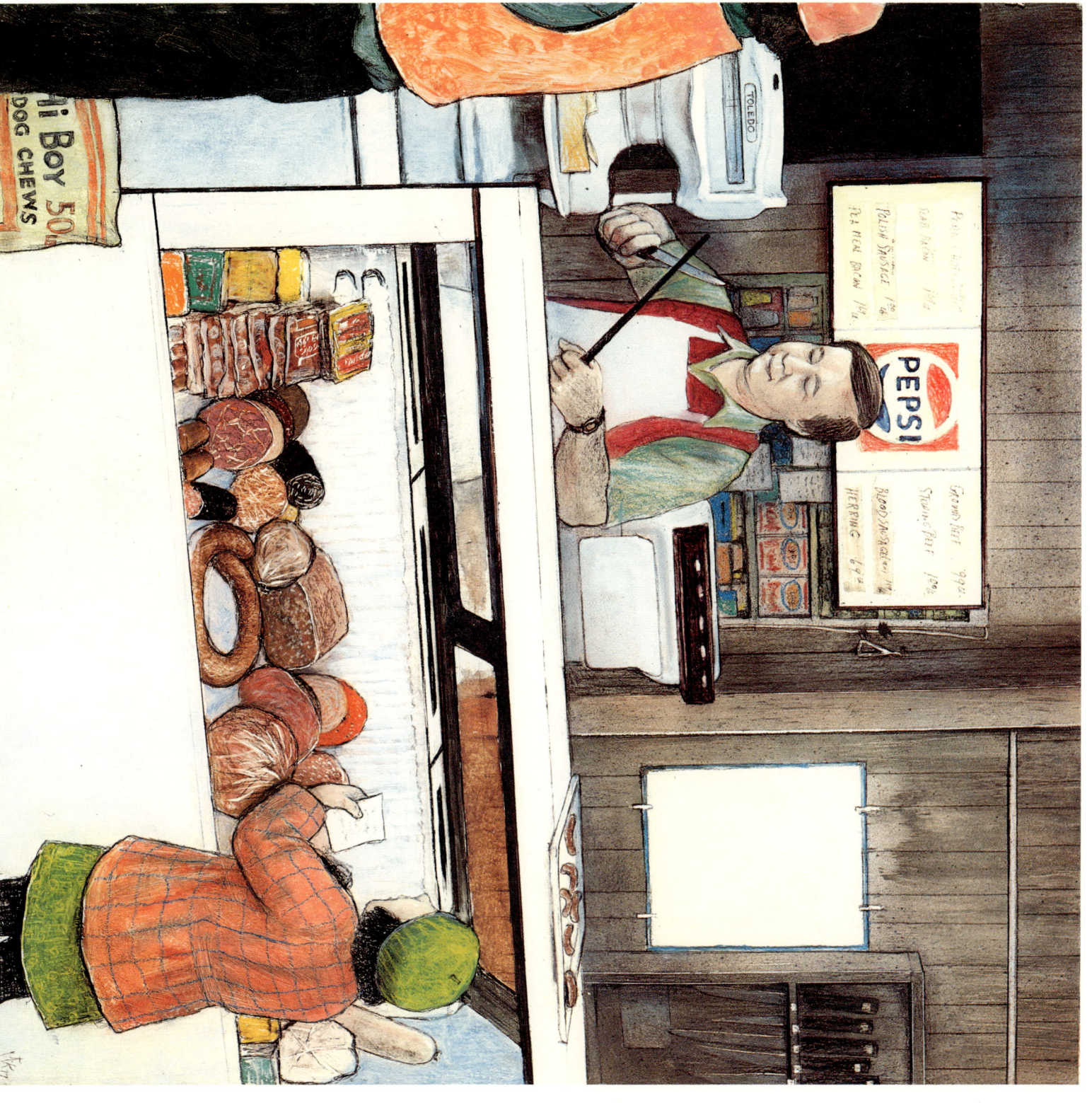

Our storekeeper, Ernie Peplinski William Kurelek

The door is always open

Rumleskie's garage in Combermere fascinated me as a possible painting subject even before I conceived the Polish series. I take my children's bikes and our garden tractor there for repairs. Willie Rumleskie has a real back-country character and a lovely Ottawa Valley dialect to go with it. He failed his first mechanics' certificate test, they say, because he couldn't read it and understand the questions on it. But when a new kind of test based on practical mechanical aptitude was substituted he passed it with first-class honors.

Actually I'm rather apprehensive in dealing with tradesmen out there because they sometimes laugh at me for being a helpless artist who has to call on others to fix things for him, or else they take advantage of my ignorance and charge me heavily for their services. But not Willie — his rates are low and he even apologizes for them.

His garage is really two old houses joined together. Ernie Peplinski, our Combermere storekeeper, was born in the back, taller one. Children in that area were often born at home in those days because their parents couldn't afford a hospital confinement for the mother. Willie's approach to repair and maintenance work is both rough-and-ready and easygoing. He has no hydraulic hoist. He works on transmissions from below in the pit I show in the painting. Willie doesn't lock the door. People drop in for a chat any time of day and the dog in the picture is always there to greet them. The yard itself is a fantastic jumble of scrap iron and broken-down machines. Thank goodness snow covered most of these details for this already intricate painting. Those Polish names were really there in the photos I took as reference material — as if to emphasize the Polishness of this series. W.K.

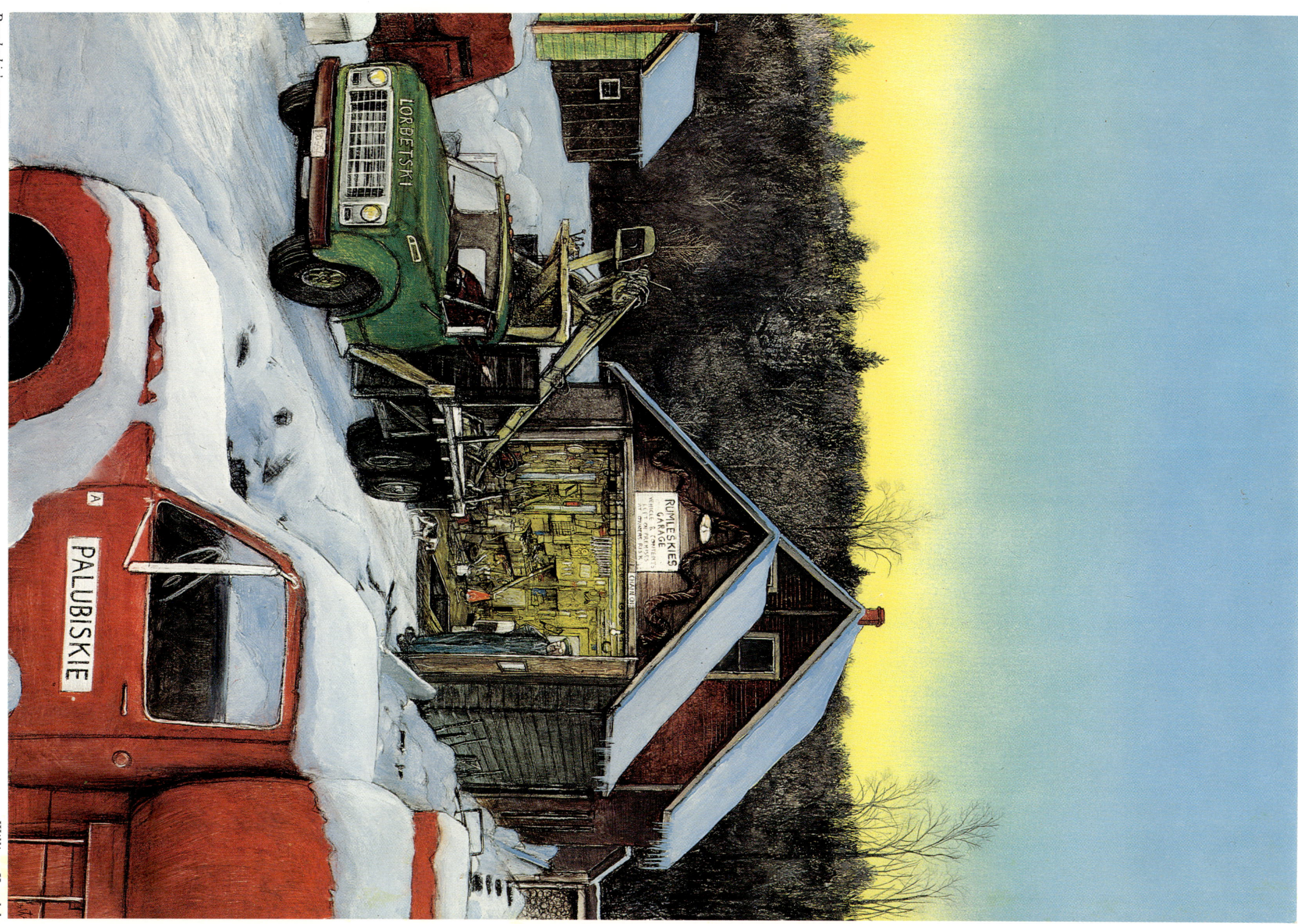

Rumleskie's garage

William Kurelek

Part seven

A long good life

Henry Chapeskie, the son of a fairly wealthy and educated landlord class settler in the Renfrew area, was born in 1895. Henry's first job after school was as a municipality clerk. Then he was elected the first reeve of Barry's Bay. He retained that position for 14 years either by election or by acclamation. He accomplished a lot for that part of Renfrew County: hydroelectrification; reforestation; building the community hospital we see in the painting. He was also into sports and music (he played the organ and taught Polish hymns). Because of his lumbering business, he employed many men at the sawmill and in the bush. He held other government offices, notably that of warden and justice of the peace.

Of his eight children, one son, Andrew, became a doctor and aviator, a daughter, Lorraine, became a pharmacist, two girls became nurses and two girls became teachers. I interviewed him at his Barry's Bay home where he is semi-retired. His booming voice is as strong as ever and he holds to original and strong views on community affairs. Tourism, for example, as he explained to me, is much too over-estimated as an industry in that area. The season is too short.

We should go back to solid old virtues. We should care for our forest land, use it without destroying it. We should return to craftsmanship. We should be content with less. W.K.

Note: Reeve Chapeskie died peacefully in his sleep in January 1981 at the age of 85. Ed.

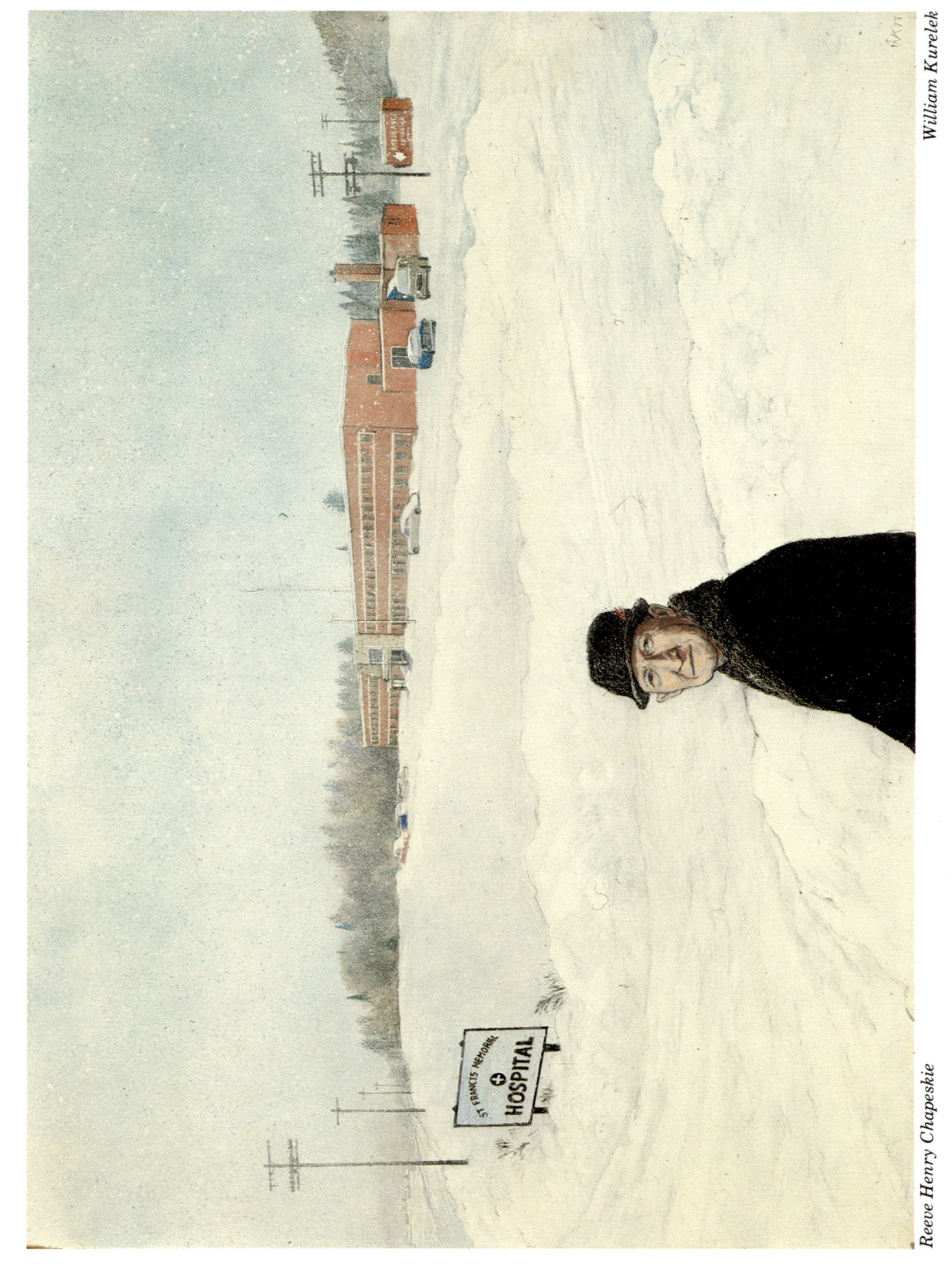

Reeve Henry Chapeskie — William Kurelek

Blessings

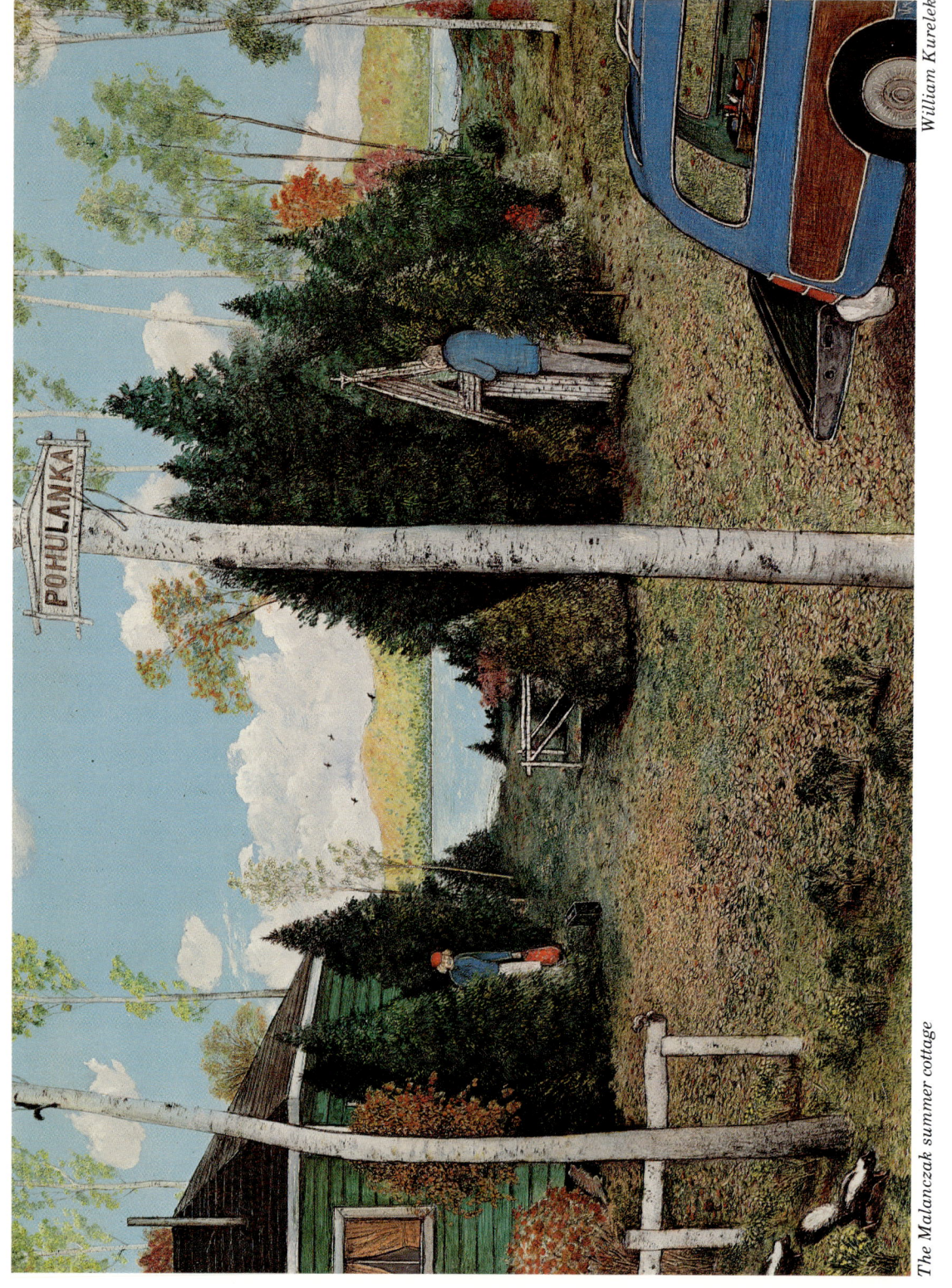

The Malanczak summer cottage — William Kurelek

A shrine in the garden

I have known Roman for some 12 years now. First I used to give him rides on my visits to Madonna House of the lay apostolate, which is not far from his cottage on Long Lake. Then I got my own farm studio near Madonna House so we're all set now to enjoy each other's company on the four-hour, 200-mile drive between Combermere and Toronto. His wife Wanda sometimes comes along and we discuss philosophy, religion and share jokes. Roman doesn't drive because of a manual handicap so he comes up to his cottage (which he's named Pohulanka after a district where he grew up in the Old Country) either by bus or with his children who have cottages next to him, or with me. I've included my car in the picture for compositional reasons, as they prepare to come back with me to Toronto.

In many of my paintings I sneak Christian symbols into the composition. I didn't need to in a picture about Roman. He is a devout Catholic and isn't ashamed to show it. Witness the wayside shrine he's made of birch branches before which he says a prayer on arriving and leaving, as his people used to do in Poland. There is a long-standing, half-playful difference between Wanda and Roman about the amount of trees and other growth there should be around the cottage. Here I've taken artist's licence and sided with Wanda by removing a lot of trees so we can get a better glimpse of the lake in the distance. There is still enough foliage to conceal some of the half dozen birds and animals indigenous to the area. Perhaps the viewer can spot them. I've chosen autumn as the time of year because of the breathtaking beauty of the country when the leaves are in full, fall color. I hasten to add it's hopeless trying to match God in artistry. W.K.

The fruit of the earth

Poles began settling in the Leduc, Nisku and through the lake areas, going as far as 50 miles south of Edmonton, Alberta, back in the 1890's. Life was very hard at first. The ability to get their produce to market was the key to success for many of those early pioneers. Leduc had a railway into Edmonton, so that eggs, butter, potatoes, milk, even fence posts, found ready sales there. Eventually that whole area prospered thanks to markets stimulated by two World Wars and the discovery of oil.

Most of these Polish pioneers like Piotr Jarosz, who eventually made good, were impoverished when they arrived. But a few were considered wealthy back in the Old Country, as for example the Hamula brothers, Michael, Joseph and Andrew, who came over in 1898. Their father, the owner of 60 morgs of good land (about 30 acres), eight horses and numerous cows, was considered by the Poles to be a rich man, able to provide good security for his sons. However, the brothers decided that a 30-acre farm was not large enough to satisfy their ambitions if divided into three parts.

Since they could do nothing but farm, they sold their shares, came to Canada, and settled in the Nisku and Leduc area on a common farm. The farm was a former Indian burial ground and thus the name "Indian" was given to it.

They built a small house, purchased two horses and two cows and were soon able to clear the land and put it under cultivation. In addition to farming they worked on the railway for $1.25 a day. After three years of hard work they were able to buy two other farms, so that they each had a farm.

With such a good beginning they were able to develop very good farms. Their children are now rich and respected citizens. W.K.

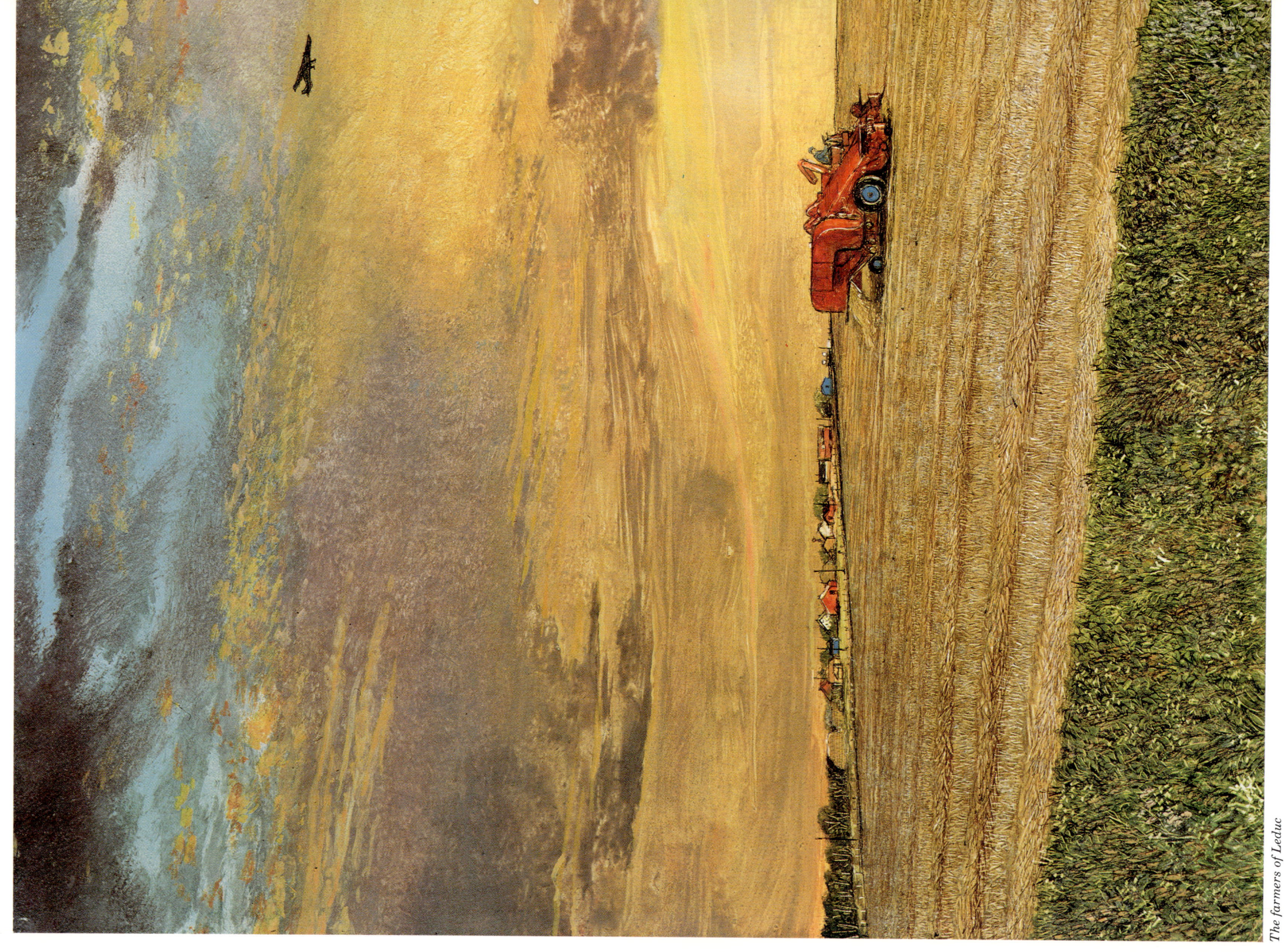

The farmers of Leduc

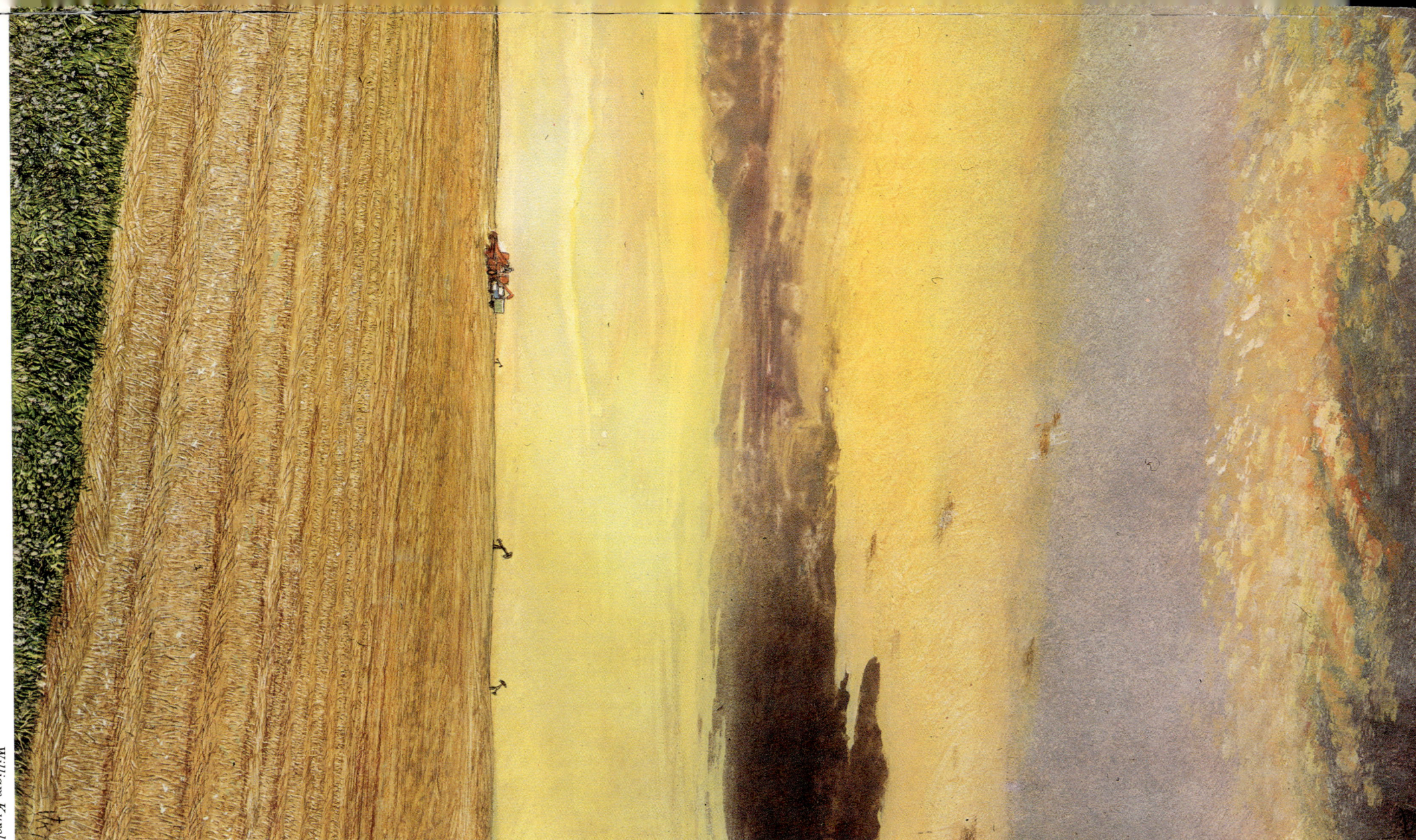

William Kurelek

A cathedral in the pines

I cannot say much about this painting except how awed and impressed I was the first summer Roman showed me this place — and that in spite of it being a dreary, wet day. The second time was in late fall. The screen depiction of Our Lady of Czestochowa (Poland's national icon — which even today is helping the people keep their independence and holy faith) was rolled up and put into storage for the winter. And yet, the natural cathedral concept in the soaring pine trees with a soft pine needle floor, still impressed me.

The chapel is used mostly by Polish boy scouts and girl guides who come from their summer camp in the Kaszuby district — also by tourists and cottagers. All places are occupied for Mass on a fair day in summer as can be seen in the National Film Board sequence on it in their film "Kaszuby." It has an isolated monastery atmosphere about it, rather than that of a parish church, because there are no towns or farms adjacent, just the forest and the lake behind. W.K.

Note: The chapel was conceived as a guidance center for youth and built by a Polish Franciscan, Father Rafal Jan Ignatius Grzondziel, in 1955-56. It is located on Lake Wadsworth between Barry's Bay, Wilno and Combermere. On one Sunday in 1966, as many as 7,000 attended Mass there. The Black Madonna is a copy of the painting at the Miracle Shrine in Czestochowa, Poland; it is believed to date from the third century and to be the oldest painting in Church history. Ed.

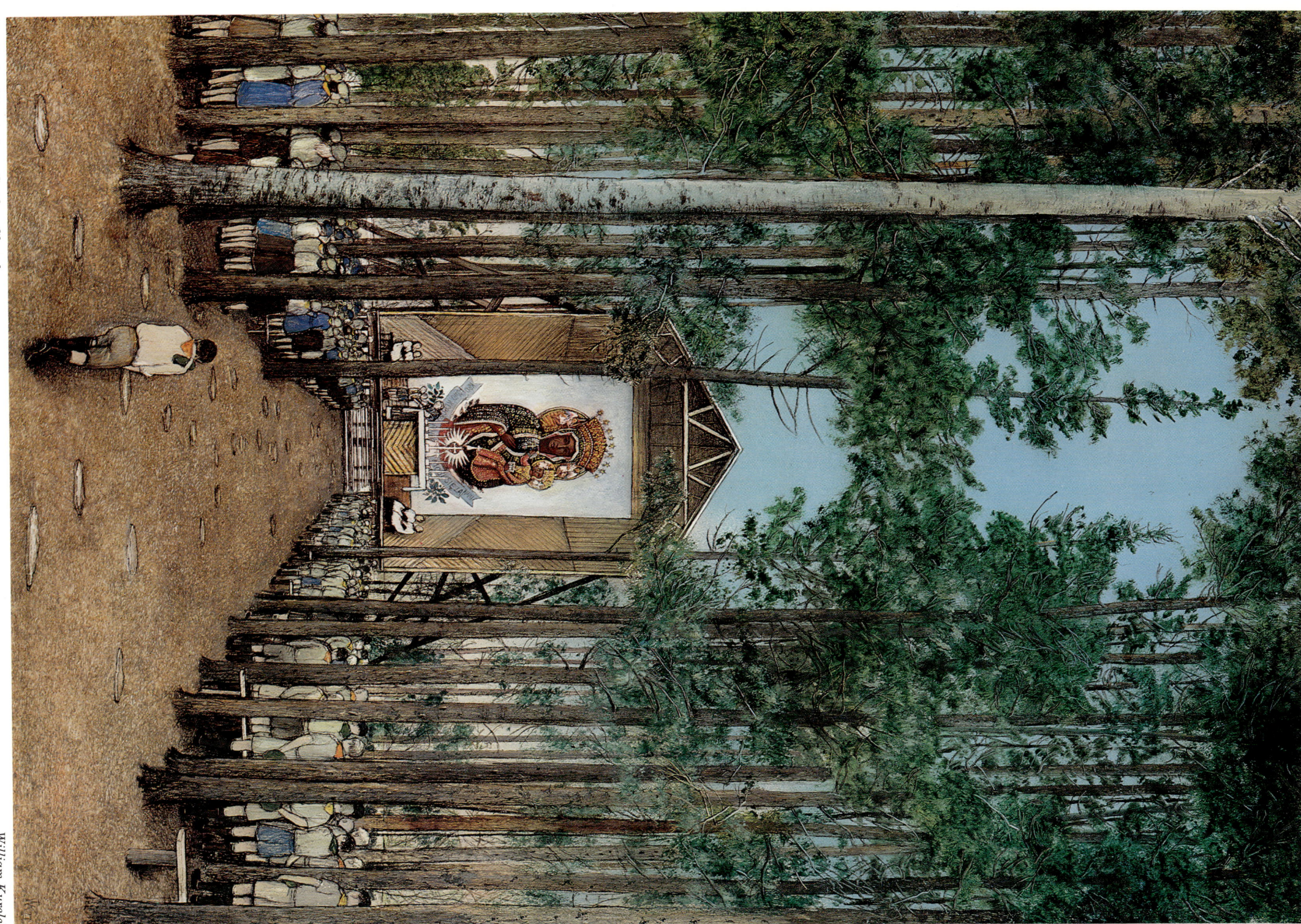

Our Lady of Czestochowa Outdoor Chapel — William Kurelek

Notes

The editor has tried to get in touch with all individuals or their descendants mentioned by name in William Kurelek's text. Each was asked to verify the facts mentioned. Because of the wide variations between Polish and English spellings of surnames, the editorial policy was to follow the spelling requested by the individual or family concerned.

4. The Polish Alliance of Canada who sponsored this series of paintings is about to celebrate its 75th anniversary. As an organization composed of people of Polish descent, it operates community centers throughout Canada and publishes the largest Polish language newspaper in the country.

6. Sir Casimir Gzowski (1813-1898) came to Canada in 1842. The information on him was taken from Makowski and from Wycliffe College files.

8. In 1967 when Makowski wrote his book, which Kurelek used as the basis for this painting, Piotr Jarosz was 93 and living in Oldegrow, B.C.

12. Polish settlement in the Lakehead gained momentum after World War I. The Polish Mutual Benefit Society was formed in 1928, and in 1930 bought an old church that became the center of the Polish community for the twin cities. Information from Makowski.

17. The lumber king referred to was J.R. Booth (1826-1925).

18. Kurelek claimed he borrowed this railway scene from Pierre Berton's book on the building of the C.P.R., but Mr. Berton says it must be a composite based on several photographs.

20. The Jósef Glista story was told to Kurelek by the late Ted Glista.

23. Information on the Polish-Irish fight was taken from Makowski.

24. The Racoski farm exists very much like this at present. The fences built from the stones cleared from the fields led one observer to say "there were enough to build many China walls."

26. Brother Anthony Kowalczyk O.M.I. is also known as Frère Antoine. The first steps in connection with his beatification were taken April 17, 1952, by the Reverend Father Giuseppe Morabito, O.M.I., postulator, and the testimony was completed June 13. Information taken from Makowski and from Oblate files. Collège Saint-Jean is now Faculté Saint-Jean, part of the University of Alberta.

28. Information from Makowski and the Public Archives, Ottawa.

32. Makowski dates this scene between 1901 and 1906. Polish immigrants formed the first Polish association in Torronto in 1907; it was called The Sons of Poland.

35. Information checked by Father J.A. Maclean, now parish priest at St. Mary's of the Nativity, Sydney, N.S.

36. According to Roman Malanczak, Kurelek used the kitchen of Mrs. A. Kosnaski as the model for this painting. Her home is situated halfway between Barry's Bay and Combermere.

39. The farm is owned by Ambrose Lehovitch (Polish spelling: Lechowicz). His wife who supplied Kurelek with information on her school days was Mary Yarascovitch before her marriage.

48. This information comes from both Makowski and from Kurelek's interview with H.J. Chapeskie. Supplemented by information from Dr. A.H. Chapeskie, Barry's Bay.

51. Roman Malanczak's cottage is at Kaszouby.

51. This information taken from Makowski was checked by Peter Hamula of Edmonton.

54. Father Grzondziel is now parish priest at the Holy Cross Polish Mission in Woodstock, Ontario. The huge painting of the Black Madonna was done first in black lines by a Polish artist Sulma; the colors were added two years later by Professor Ugo Chyurlia of Rome University. The chapel is used by Hungarian scouts as well as Polish.